Taste of Home

Meat & Potato

Lover's Cookbook

Slow-Cooked Sirloin (p. 13)

Meat-and-Potato Lovers, Rejoice!

FINALLY...a cookbook that isn't afraid to call it like it is! *The Meat & Potato Lover's Cookbook* offers only the beefy main courses and hearty potato side dishes that are just perfect for the steak-and-spud fanatic in your home.

Take a look inside and you will find more than 250 lip-smacking, finger-licking favorites shared by family cooks from coast to coast. You'll enjoy nothing but traditional tastes from this collection. No hard-to-find ingredients, no hard-to-follow directions, nothing but down-home staples that taste so great, they are sure to spur many requests for second helpings.

This cookbook highlights dishes that stood the test of time. Classic pot roasts, flame-broiled steaks and old-fashioned meat loaves are only a sampling of the treasured recipes you'll discover among this mouth-watering assortment.

Ground beef casseroles that are bubbling with stick-to-your-ribs goodness, heart-warming stews featuring tender chunks of beef and other meaty, meal-in-one specialties are also included. In addition, you'll find saucy meatball hoagies, spicy sausage jambalayas and pizzas piled high with pepperoni and other savory toppings.

And since man cannot live on meat alone (or can he?), you are invited to pair the steaks, roasts and tenderloins with any of the dozens of potato side dishes found in the chapter "Spuds on the Side" (p. 38). You will also find a few popular potato favorites in chapters such as "Grilled Greats" (p. 58), "Other Specialties" (p. 94) and, of course, "One-Dish Dinners" (p. 20).

All you have to do is sink your teeth into any of the fantastic dishes offered here and you'll see why this book is sure to become one of your most trusted kitchen tools. Assembled by *Taste of Home*, America's No. 1 recipe source, *Meat & Potato Lover's Cookbook* is sure to keep satisfying everyone at your supper table for years to come.

Editor: Mark Hagen
Art Directors: Gretchen Trautman, Edwin Robles
Layout Designer: Emma Acevedo
Vice President, Executive Editor/Books: Heidi Reuter Lloyd
Associate Editors: Sara Lancaster, Jean Steiner
Proofreader: Linne Bruskewitz
Editorial Assistant: Barb Czysz

Food Director: Diane Werner, RD
Test Kitchen Manager: Karen Scales
Recipe Editors: Sue A. Jurack (Senior), Mary King, Christine Rukavena
Recipe Asset System Manager: Coleen Martin
Home Economists: Tina Johnson, Marie Parker, Annie Rose
Test Kitchen Assistant: Rita Krajcir

Studio Photographers: Rob Hagen (Senior), Dan Roberts, Jim Wieland, Lori Foy
Senior Food Stylists: Sarah Thompson, Joylyn Trickel
Food Stylist Assistants: Kaitlyn Basasie, Alynna Malson
Set Stylists: Jennifer Bradley Vent (Senior), Dee Dee Schaefer, Stephanie Marchese
Photo Studio Coordinator: Kathleen Swaney

Creative Director: Ardyth Cope
Senior Vice President, Editor in Chief: Catherine Cassidy
President: Barbara Newton
Founder: Roy Reiman

©2007 Reiman Media Group, Inc.
5400 S. 60th Street, Greendale WI 53129

International Standard Book Number (10): 0-89821-589-7
International Standard Book Number (13): 978-0-89821-589-2
Library of Congress Control Number: 2007925267
All rights reserved. Printed in U.S.A.

For other *Taste of Home* books
and products, visit *www.shoptasteofhome.com*.

Cover photo of Steak Diane (p. 14) and Zucchini Twice-Baked Potatoes (p. 57) by Rob Hagen. Food styled by Joylyn Trickel and Sara Thompson. Set styled by Stephanie Marchese.

Taste of Home
Meat & Potato
Lover's Cookbook

Beef Tenderloin with Potatoes (p.

Meat & Potato Lover's Cookbook

Chapter 1

Meaty Entrees

Savory meat loaves...slow-cooked favorites...tender fall-off-the-bone ribs...when you're hankering for a hearty meal that will satisfy the biggest appetite, you can't go wrong with any of these meaty "main attractions."

Greek-Style Rib Eye Steaks

Greek-Style Rib Eye Steaks

Ruby Williams, Bogalusa, Louisiana

Because our children are grown, I often cook for just my husband and me. When I want to serve something special, this is the entree I usually reach for. Black olives and feta cheese give the steak such great flavor.

- 1-1/2 teaspoons garlic powder
- 1-1/2 teaspoons dried oregano
- 1-1/2 teaspoons dried basil
- 1/2 teaspoon salt
- 1/8 teaspoon pepper
- 2 boneless beef rib eye steaks (1-1/2 inches thick and 8 ounces *each*)
- 1 tablespoon olive oil
- 1 tablespoon lemon juice
- 2 tablespoons crumbled feta cheese
- 1 tablespoon sliced ripe olives

In a small bowl, combine the first five ingredients; rub onto both sides of steaks. In a large skillet, cook steaks in oil for 7-9 minutes on each side or until meat reaches desired doneness (for medium-rare a meat thermometer should read 145°; medium, 160°; well-done, 170°). Sprinkle with lemon juice, cheese and olives. Serve immediately.
Yield: 2 servings.

Santa Fe Strip Steaks

Joan Hallford, North Richland Hills, Texas

We love food with a Southwestern flair, and this recipe certainly provides it. Green chilies, jalapeno pepper and a zesty blend of seasonings give it the right amount of kick.

✔ *Uses less fat, sugar or salt. Includes Nutrition Facts.*

- 1/2 cup chopped onion
- 1 tablespoon olive oil
- 2 cans (4 ounces *each*) chopped green chilies
- 1/2 cup fresh cilantro leaves
- 1 jalapeno pepper, seeded
- 2 teaspoons red currant jelly
- 1 teaspoon chicken bouillon granules
- 1 teaspoon Worcestershire sauce
- 1 garlic clove, peeled
- 1/2 teaspoon seasoned salt
- 1/4 teaspoon dried oregano
- 4 New York strip steaks (about 1 inch thick and 7 ounces *each*)

Salt and pepper to taste

- 1/2 cup shredded Monterey Jack cheese, optional

In a small saucepan, saute onion in oil until tender. Transfer to a blender or food processor. Add the green chilies, cilantro, jalapeno, jelly, bouillon, Worcestershire sauce, garlic, seasoned salt and oregano; cover and process until smooth. Return mixture to the saucepan. Bring to a boil. Reduce heat; simmer, uncovered, for 10 minutes. Set aside and keep warm.

Sprinkle steaks with salt and pepper. Broil 4-6 in. from heat for 4-8 minutes on each side or until meat reaches desired doneness (for medium-rare, a meat thermometer should read 145°; medium, 160°; well-done, 170°). Serve steaks with green chili sauce and sprinkle with cheese if desired.
Yield: 4 servings.

Nutrition Facts: 1 serving (calculated with salt and pepper) equals 457 calories, 31 g fat (11 g saturated fat), 109 mg cholesterol, 727 mg sodium, 8 g carbohydrate, 2 g fiber, 36 g protein.

Editor's Note: Steaks may also be grilled, uncovered, over medium heat. When cutting or seeding hot peppers, use rubber or plastic gloves to protect your hands. Avoid touching your face. Steak may be known as strip steak, Kansas City steak, New York Strip steak, Ambassador Steak or boneless Club Steak in your region.

Santa Fe Strip Steaks

Onion-Smothered Sirloins

Tina Michalicka, Hudson, Florida

Friends and family love these savory steaks and sweet onions. Featuring ingredients I almost always happen to have on hand, the dinner is simple to prepare. It is constantly well received. For spicier steaks, you can increase the pepper flakes and cumin.

- 1 teaspoon garlic powder
- 3/4 teaspoon salt, *divided*
- 1/2 teaspoon ground cumin
- 1/2 teaspoon dried oregano
- 1/4 teaspoon crushed red pepper flakes
- 4 boneless beef sirloin steaks (about 1 inch thick and 8 ounces *each*)
- 2 large sweet onions, cut into 1/2-inch slices and separated into rings
- 1/4 cup olive oil
- 1/4 teaspoon pepper
- 1 medium lime, cut into quarters

In a bowl, combine the garlic powder, 1/2 teaspoon salt, cumin, oregano and pepper flakes. Rub over the steaks; set aside.

Place onions in a disposable foil pan; add oil and toss to coat. Grill, covered, over medium heat for 30-40 minutes or until golden brown, stirring occasionally. Season onions with pepper, remaining salt and a squeeze of lime.

Grill the steaks, uncovered, over medium heat for 7-10 minutes on each side or until a meat reaches desired doneness (for medium-rare, a meat thermometer should read 145°; medium, 160°; well-done, 170°). Squeeze remaining lime over the steaks; top with onions. **Yield:** 4 servings.

Onion-Smothered Sirloins

Sirloin with Bernaise Sauce

Willa Govoro, Nevada, Missouri

When I want a meal that's extraordinary, I feature this beef roast as the centerpiece. The pale yellow sauce with flecks of green looks lovely draped over the slices.

- 1/2 teaspoon garlic salt
- 1/2 teaspoon pepper
- 1 boneless beef sirloin roast (5 to 6 pounds)

BERNAISE SAUCE

- 1/4 cup white wine vinegar
- 1/2 cup chopped green onions
- 1 tablespoon minced fresh tarragon *or* 1 teaspoon dried tarragon
- 1/4 teaspoon pepper
- 4 egg yolks, lightly beaten
- 1 tablespoon cold water
- 1/4 teaspoon salt
- 1/8 teaspoon cayenne pepper
- 3/4 cup cold butter
- 1 tablespoon minced fresh parsley

Combine garlic salt and pepper; rub over roast. Place on a rack in a shallow roasting pan. Bake, uncovered, at 350° for 2-1/2 to 3 hours or until meat reaches desired doneness (for medium-rare, a meat thermometer should read 145°; medium, 160°; well-done, 170°). Let stand for 10-15 minutes before slicing.

Meanwhile, in a saucepan, combine the vinegar, onions, tarragon and pepper; bring to a boil. Strain, reserving liquid; discard onions and tarragon.

Place egg yolks in a heavy saucepan. Gradually whisk in water, vinegar mixture, salt and cayenne. Cook until the mixture begins to thicken, stirring constantly. Add butter, 1 tablespoon at a time, until the mixture has thickened and reaches 160°, stirring constantly. Remove from the heat; stir in parsley. Serve warm with sliced beef. **Yield:** 12 servings.

Sirloin with Bernaise Sauce

Mushroom Beef Patties

Stuffed Meat Loaf

Lisa Williams, Steamboat Springs, Colorado

My husband's job takes him away from home a good deal. When he returns, his first request is always for this savory, stuffed meat loaf featuring a delicious cheese and veggie filling.

1-1/4	pounds lean ground beef
1	pound bulk hot sausage
1-1/2	cups herb-seasoned dry bread stuffing
1	egg, beaten
5	tablespoons ketchup, *divided*
3	tablespoons steak sauce, *divided*
1	cup (4 ounces) shredded cheddar cheese
1	small tomato, diced
1	small onion, diced
1/2	small green pepper, diced
8	to 10 fresh mushrooms, sliced
4	ounces thinly sliced fully cooked ham, optional
1	cup (4 ounces) shredded Swiss cheese

In a mixing bowl, combine the ground beef, sausage, stuffing, egg, 3 tablespoons ketchup and 2 tablespoons steak sauce. Mix well.

Pat half of the meat mixture into a 9-in. x 5-in. x 2-in. loaf pan. Sprinkle with cheddar cheese. Layer with tomato, onion, green pepper, mushrooms, ham if desired and Swiss cheese. Cover with remaining meat mixture; press down firmly to seal. (Mixture may be higher than the top of the pan.)

Combine remaining ketchup and steak sauce; drizzle over top of meat loaf. Bake at 350° for 1 hour or until no pink remains, draining off fat when necessary. **Yield:** 6-8 servings.

Mushroom Beef Patties

Dale Thelen, Bedford, Texas

Even though I'm a "city boy," my co-workers have said I'm the most country city boy they have ever run across. Maybe that's because of the comforting, hearty recipes I share, like this ground beef dish.

2	tablespoons milk
1	tablespoon Worcestershire sauce
1/4	cup dry bread crumbs
1	teaspoon salt, *divided*
1/2	teaspoon pepper
1/2	teaspoon garlic powder
1	pound ground beef
1/2	pound sliced fresh mushrooms
1	teaspoon dried basil
5	tablespoons butter, *divided*
2	tablespoons all-purpose flour
1/2	cup half-and-half cream
1/2	to 3/4 cup water
1/4	teaspoon hot pepper sauce
1/4	cup shredded cheddar cheese
2	tablespoons chopped green onions

In a bowl, combine the milk, Worcestershire sauce, bread crumbs, 1/2 teaspoon salt, pepper and garlic powder. Crumble beef over mixture and mix well. Shape into three or four oval patties. In a large skillet, cook patties over medium heat until no longer pink.

In another skillet, saute mushrooms and basil in 2 tablespoons butter until tender; drain. Remove mushrooms with a slotted spoon and set aside.

In the same skillet, melt the remaining butter; stir in flour until smooth. Gradually whisk in the cream, 1/2 cup water, pepper sauce and remaining salt. Bring to a boil; cook and stir for 2 minutes or until thickened and bubbly. Add enough remaining water to make a medium-thin sauce. Add reserved mushrooms; heat though. Serve over beef patties; top with cheese and onions. **Yield:** 3-4 servings.

Beef Tenderloin with Potatoes

Beef Tenderloin With Potatoes

Mrs. Clifford Davis, Fort Smith, Arkansas

As an alternative to turkey or ham for the holidays one year, I decided to try this recipe. My family liked it so much, it's become a standard at our house. The meat is very tender and flavorful, and the potatoes become nicely browned.

2-1/4   cups water
1-1/2   cups ketchup
   3   envelopes (.7 ounce *each*) Italian salad dressing mix
   1   tablespoon prepared mustard
 3/4   teaspoon Worcestershire sauce
   1   whole beef tenderloin (3 to 4 pounds), trimmed
 10   medium potatoes, peeled and quarters
 1/2   cup butter, melted
 1/2   teaspoon salt
 1/4   teaspoon pepper

Combine the first five ingredients in a large resealable plastic bag. Pierce tenderloin in several places; place in bag and turn to coat. Seal and refrigerate for 8 hours or overnight.

Place potatoes in a large saucepan and cover with water. Bring to a boil; cook for 10-15 minutes or until crisp-tender; drain. Toss with butter, salt and pepper.

Place tenderloin on a rack in a roasting pan. Pour marinade into saucepan; bring to a rolling boil. Boil for 1 minute; pour over meat. Arrange the potatoes around meat.

Bake, uncovered, at 375° for 60-75 minutes, basting occasionally, or until beef reaches desired doneness (for medium-rare, a meat thermometer should read 145°; medium, 160°; well-done, 170°). Slice; serve with pan juices and potatoes. **Yield:** 10-12 servings.

Stuffed Flank Steak

Bernice McFadden, Dayton, Ohio

This is one of my favorite beef recipes. Tasty, juicy and tucked full of vegetables, it warms up chilly nights.

   1   beef flank steak (about 1-1/4 pounds)
 1/2   cup soy sauce
 1/4   cup vegetable oil
   2   tablespoons molasses
   2   teaspoons ground mustard
   1   teaspoon ground ginger
   1   garlic cloves, minced
1-1/2   cups cooked long grain rice
   1   medium carrot, shredded
 1/2   cup sliced water chestnuts
 1/4   cup sliced green onions

Starting along one long side, cut a horizontal slit through the steak to within 1/2 in. of the opposite side. Place steak in a greased 13-in. x 9-in. x 2-in. baking dish. Combine the soy sauce, oil, molasses, mustard, ginger and garlic; set aside 1/4 cup. Pour the remaining marinade over the meat. Let stand for 30 minutes.

Meanwhile, combine the rice, carrot, water chestnuts, onions and reserved marinade. Stuff into steak. Cover and bake at 350° for 45 minutes.

Uncover; baste with pan drippings. Bake 15-20 minutes longer or until meat is tender. Brush again with pan drippings if desired. **Yield:** 4 servings.

Round Steak Supper

Sandra Castillo, Janesville, Wisconsin

Here's a meat-and-potatoes dinner that will help you stick to your budget. Inexpensive round steak and potatoes are simmered for hours in an onion-flavored gravy to create the satisfying supper.

   4   large potatoes, peeled and cut into 1/2-inch cubes
1-1/2   pounds boneless beef round steak
   1   can (10-3/4 ounces) condensed cream of mushroom soup, undiluted
 1/2   cup water
   1   envelope onion soup mix
Pepper and garlic powder to taste

Place the potatoes in a 3-qt. slow cooker. Cut beef into four pieces; place over potatoes. In a bowl, combine the soup, water, soup mix, pepper and garlic powder. Pour over the beef.

Cover and cook on low for 6-8 hours or until meat and potatoes are tender. **Yield:** 4 servings.

Stuffed Flank Steak

Mushroom Strip Steaks

Mushroom Strip Steaks

Kay Riedel, Topeka, Kansas

When you want to dress up steak in a hurry, try this easy and tasty idea. My husband and I enjoy the succulent combination of beef, mushrooms, cheese and onion soup featured in this satisfying recipe.

> 2 boneless New York strip steaks (about 1/2 pound)
> 1 to 2 tablespoons vegetable oil
> 1 can (10-1/2 ounces) condensed French onion soup, undiluted
> 1 jar (6 ounces) sliced mushrooms, drained
> 1/2 cup shredded part-skim mozzarella cheese

In a large skillet over medium-high heat, cook the steaks in oil for 4-6 minutes on each side or until a meat reaches desired doneness (for medium-rare, a meat thermometer should read 145°; medium, 160°; well-done, 170°). Drain.

Top each steak with the soup, mushrooms and mozzarella cheese. Cover and cook for 2-4 minutes or until the cheese is melted. **Yield:** 2 servings.

Editor's Note: Steak may be known as strip steak, Kansas City steak, New York Strip steak, Ambassador Steak or boneless Club Steak in your region.

Meat-and-Potato Patties

Gladys Klein, Burlington, Wisconsin

During World War II, when meat was rationed and had to be purchased with tokens, this recipe went a long way in feeding a family. To this day, I still reach for it whenever I want something different from regular hamburgers.

> 3/4 pound lean ground beef
> 3/4 cup finely shredded potatoes
> 1/4 cup finely chopped onion
> 2 tablespoons chopped green pepper
> 1 egg, beaten
> 1/4 teaspoon salt
> 1 tablespoon vegetable oil
> 1 cup tomato juice
> 1 tablespoon all-purpose flour
> 1/4 cup water

In a large mixing bowl, combine beef, potatoes, onion, green pepper, egg and salt. Shape into four flat patties.

Heat oil in a skillet. Brown the patties on both sides; drain. Add tomato juice. Simmer 20-25 minutes or until meat is no longer pink. Remove patties to a serving platter; keep warm.

Combine flour and water; gradually add to juice in the skillet. Cook over medium-low heat, stirring constantly until thickened. Spoon over patties. Serve immediately. **Yield:** 4 servings.

Breaded Sirloin

Sandra Lee Pippin, Aurora, Colorado

The savory breading keeps this entree deliciously tender and packed with flavor. I know your family will enjoy this main course just as much as mine does!

> 2 eggs
> 1/2 cup milk
> 1 cup seasoned bread crumbs
> 3 tablespoons grated Parmesan cheese
> 2 tablespoons minced fresh parsley
> 2 garlic cloves, minced
> 1/4 teaspoon salt
> 1/8 teaspoon pepper
> 2 pounds boneless beef sirloin steak (1-1/2 inches thick), cut into eight pieces
> 1/4 cup vegetable oil
> 4 medium ripe tomatoes, sliced
> 8 slices part-skim mozzarella cheese

Lemon wedges

In a shallow bowl, whisk the eggs and milk. In another shallow bowl, combine the bread crumbs, Parmesan cheese, parsley, garlic, salt and pepper. Dip steak in egg mixture, then roll in crumb mixture.

In a skillet over medium-high heat, cook steaks in oil in batches for 2-3 minutes on each side or until meat is no longer pink. Drain on paper towels.

Transfer to an ungreased baking sheet. Top beef with tomato and cheese slices. Broil 4-6 in. from the heat for 1-2 minutes or until cheese is melted. Serve with lemon. **Yield:** 8 servings.

Breaded Sirloin

Cajun Pepper Steak

Cajun Pepper Steak

Martha Sue Kinnaird, Ruston, Louisiana

Cajun recipes have become popular across the country, but they've always been loved here. See if this recipe doesn't become a family favorite at your house.

1-1/2 **pounds boneless round steak, cut into cubes**
  2 **tablespoons vegetable oil**
  1 **can (14-1/2 ounces) beef broth**
  1 **can (14-1/2 ounces) diced tomatoes, undrained**
  1 **cup chopped green pepper**
1/2 **cup chopped onion**
  3 **garlic cloves, minced**
  2 **teaspoons Worcestershire sauce**
  1 **bay leaf**
1/2 **teaspoon dried basil**
1/4 **to 1/2 teaspoon Cajun seasoning**
1/8 **teaspoon salt**
1/8 **teaspoon pepper**
  2 **tablespoons cornstarch**
  2 **tablespoons cold water**
Hot cooked rice *or* noodles

In a large skillet, cook beef in oil over medium heat until browned; drain. Stir in the broth, tomatoes, green pepper, onion, garlic, Worcestershire sauce and seasonings. Bring to a boil; reduce heat. Cover and simmer for 1 hour or until meat is tender.

Discard bay leaf. Combine the cornstarch and water until smooth; stir into meat mixture. Bring meat mixture to a boil; cook and stir for 2 minutes or until thickened. Serve over rice or noodles. **Yield:** 4-6 servings.

Beef Steaks with Blue Cheese

Gloria Nerone, Mentor, Ohio

My guests often ask for this winning recipe and are surprised at how simple it is to put together. Blue cheese gives the steaks a mouth-watering, robust flavor.

  2 **beef tenderloin steaks, 1-1/2 inches thick**
  2 **ounces blue cheese, crumbled**
  2 **tablespoons butter, softened**
  2 **slices white bread, crusts removed and cut into cubes**
  1 **tablespoon olive oil**
  2 **tablespoons grated Parmesan cheese**

Place meat on broiler pan. Broil 4-6 in. from the heat for 5-8 minutes on each side or until meat is browned and cooked to desired doneness (for medium-rare, a meat thermometer should read 145°; medium, 160°; well-done, 170°).

Meanwhile, in a bowl, combine the blue cheese and butter; set aside. In a skillet, saute bread cubes in oil until they are golden brown. Sprinkle with Parmesan cheese. Top the steaks with blue cheese mixture and sprinkle with croutons; broil steaks 1 minute longer or until the cheese is slightly melted. **Yield:** 2 servings.

Barbecue Beef Patties

Marlene Harguth, Maynard, Minnesota

I like to fix these family-pleasing patties that taste like individual meat loaves. Barbecue sauce brushed on top makes them irresistible. Because they're so simple to make, you won't mind if your family requests them often.

  1 **egg**
1/2 **cup barbecue sauce, *divided***
3/4 **cup crushed cornflakes**
1/2 **to 1 teaspoon salt**
  1 **pound ground beef**

In a bowl, combine egg, 1/4 cup barbecue sauce, cornflake crumbs and salt. Add beef and mix well. Shape into four oval patties, about 3/4 in. thick.

Place in a greased 11-in. x 7-in. x 2-in. baking pan. Spread with remaining barbecue sauce.

Bake, uncovered, at 375° for 25-30 minutes or until meat is no longer pink and meat thermometer reads 160°; drain. **Yield:** 4 servings.

Quick Tip

For extra flair, when preparing the recipe for Barbecue Beef Patties, try mixing just a little bit of honey into the barbecue sauce.

Beef Steaks with Blue Cheese

Pepper Patties

Pepper Patties

For a tasty twist, try fixing beef burgers and colorful peppers. Our home economists suggest serving them on a bed of hot cooked noodles for a hearty dinner, alone for a lighter meal or on bread as an open-faced sandwich.

- 2 tablespoons soy sauce
- 1/4 teaspoon garlic powder
- 1/4 teaspoon pepper
- 1 pound ground beef
- 1 teaspoon vegetable oil
- 1 small onion, sliced
- 1 small green pepper, julienned
- 1 small sweet red pepper, julienned

Hot cooked noodles, optional

In a large bowl, combine the soy sauce, garlic powder and pepper; reserve 1 tablespoon and set aside. Crumble beef over the remaining soy sauce mixture; mix well. Shape into four 1/2-in.-thick patties.

In a large skillet, saute onion and peppers in oil and reserved soy sauce mixture for 3-4 minutes or until crisp-tender. Remove and set aside.

Add patties to skillet; cook, uncovered for 4-5 minutes on each side or until a meat thermometer reaches 160°; drain. Top patties with peppers and onion; cook until heated through. Serve patties over noodles if desired. **Yield:** 4 servings.

Meat Loaf Potato Surprise

Lois Edwards, Citrus Heights, California

Although I'm retired after years of teaching school, my days continue to be full. So, easy dishes like this still are a blessing to me. My husband—who's a meat loaf lover—really appreciates this recipe.

- 1 cup soft bread crumbs
- 1/2 cup beef broth
- 1 egg, beaten
- 4 teaspoons dried minced onion
- 1 teaspoon salt
- 1/4 teaspoon Italian seasoning
- 1/4 teaspoon pepper
- 1-1/2 pounds ground beef
- 4 cups frozen shredded hash brown potatoes, thawed
- 1/3 cup grated Parmesan cheese
- 1/4 cup minced fresh parsley
- 1 teaspoon onion salt

SAUCE

- 1 can (8 ounces) tomato sauce
- 1/4 cup beef broth
- 2 teaspoons prepared mustard

Additional Parmesan cheese, optional

In a bowl, combine crumbs, broth, egg and seasonings; let stand for 2 minutes. Add the beef and mix well. On a piece of waxed paper, pat meat mixture into a 10-in. square. Combine hash browns, cheese, parsley and onion salt; spoon over meat.

Roll up, jelly-roll style, removing waxed paper as you roll. Pinch edges and ends to seal; place with seam side down in an ungreased shallow baking pan.

Bake at 375° for 40 minutes. Combine the first three sauce ingredients; spoon over loaf. Return to the oven for 10 minutes. Sprinkle with Parmesan if desired. **Yield:** 8 servings.

Quick Tip

Inexpensive plastic gloves are a great way to keep your hands clean while mixing meat loaf. They're lightweight and disposable, making cleanup a snap.

Meat Loaf Potato Surprise

Slow Cooker Beef Au Jus

Slow-Cooked Sirloin

Vicki Tormaschy, Dickinson, North Dakota

My family of five likes to eat beef, so this recipe is a favorite. I usually serve it with homemade bread or rolls to soak up the tasty gravy. Add some veggies for a complete dinner.

✓ *Uses less fat, sugar or salt. Includes Nutrition Facts and Diabetic Exchanges.*

- 1 **boneless beef sirloin steak (1-1/2 pounds)**
- 1 **medium onion, cut into 1-inch chunks**
- 1 **medium green pepper, cut into 1-inch chunks**
- 1 **can (14-1/2 ounces) reduced-sodium beef broth**
- 1/4 **cup Worcestershire sauce**
- 1/4 **teaspoon dill weed**
- 1/4 **teaspoon dried thyme**
- 1/4 **teaspoon pepper**

Dash crushed red pepper flakes

- 2 **tablespoons cornstarch**
- 2 **tablespoons water**

In a large nonstick skillet coated with nonstick cooking spray, brown beef on both sides. Place onion and green pepper in a 3-qt. slow cooker. Top with beef. Combine the broth, Worcestershire sauce, dill, thyme, pepper and pepper flakes; pour over beef. Cover and cook on high for 3-4 hours or until meat reaches desired doneness and vegetables are crisp-tender.

Remove beef and keep warm. Combine cornstarch and water until smooth; gradually stir into cooking juices. Cover and cook about 30 minutes longer or until slightly thickened. Return beef to the slow cooker; heat through. **Yield:** 6 servings.

Nutrition Facts: 1 serving equals 199 calories, 6 g fat (2 g saturated fat), 68 mg cholesterol, 305 mg sodium, 8 g carbohydrate, 1 g fiber, 26 g protein. **Diabetic Exchanges:** 3 lean meat, 1 vegetable.

Slow-Cooked Sirloin

Savory Braised Beef

Eva Knight, Nashua, New Hampshire

Everyone will enjoy this delicious dish. With meat, potatoes and other vegetables, it's an unbeatable meal in itself.

✓ *Uses less fat, sugar or salt. Includes Nutrition Facts.*

- 1/2 **pound boneless beef chuck roast**
- 3/4 **cup water**
- 1 **small apple, thinly sliced**
- 1 **small onion, thinly sliced**
- 1/4 **teaspoon salt-free seasoning blend**
- 1/4 **teaspoon pepper**
- 4 **small new potatoes, halved**
- 2 **cabbage wedges (about 2 inches thick)**
- 1 **can (14-1/2 ounces) no-salt added stewed tomatoes**
- 1-1/2 **teaspoons cornstarch**
- 1-1/2 **teaspoons water**

Trim fat from meat and cut into 1-in. cubes; brown in a skillet coated with nonstick cooking spray. Add water, apple, onion, seasoning blend and pepper. Cover and simmer for 1-1/4 hours.

Add potatoes and cabbage; cover and simmer for 35 minutes or until vegetables are tender. Stir in tomatoes; cover and simmer for 10 minutes. Blend cornstarch and water; stir into skillet. Bring to a boil; cook and stir for 2 minutes. **Yield:** 2 servings.

Nutrition Facts: 1 serving equals 469 calories, 11 g fat (0 saturated fat), 75 mg cholesterol, 94 mg sodium, 68 g carbohydrate, 13 g fiber, 30 g protein.

Slow Cooker Beef Au Jus

Carol Hille, Grand Junction, Colorado

It's easy to fix this roast, which has lots of onion flavor. Sometimes I also add cubed potatoes and baby carrots to the slow cooker to make a terrific supper plus leftovers.

✓ *Uses less fat, sugar or salt. Includes Nutrition Facts and Diabetic Exchanges.*

- 1 **boneless beef rump roast (3 pounds)**
- 1 **large onion, sliced**
- 3/4 **cup reduced-sodium beef broth**
- 1 **envelope (1 ounce) au jus gravy mix**
- 2 **garlic cloves, halved**
- 1/4 **teaspoon pepper**

Cut roast in half. In a large nonstick skillet coated with nonstick cooking spray, brown meat on all sides over medium-high heat.

Place onion in a 5-qt. slow cooker. Top with meat. Combine the broth, gravy mix, garlic and pepper; pour over meat. Cover and cook on low for 6-7 hours or until meat and onion are tender.

Remove meat to a cutting board. Let stand for 10 minutes. Thinly slice meat and return to the slow cooker; serve with pan juices and onion. **Yield:** 10 servings.

Nutrition Facts: 3 ounces cooked beef with 1/4 cup pan juices equals 188 calories, 7 g fat (2 g saturated fat), 82 mg cholesterol, 471 mg sodium, 3 g carbohydrate, trace fiber, 28 g protein. **Diabetic Exchange:** 3 lean meat.

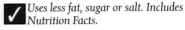
Steak Diane

Broiled Sirloin

Sue Ross, Casa Grande, Arizona

Serve this succulent beef with fluffy mashed potatoes, fresh greens and crusty bread—it's a meal fit for company! Best of all, it takes very little time to prepare.

✓ Uses less fat, sugar or salt. Includes Nutrition Facts.

- 3 **pounds beef sirloin *or* round steak (about 1 inch thick)**
- 1 **medium onion, chopped**
- 1/2 **cup lemon juice**
- 1/4 **cup vegetable oil**
- 1 **teaspoon garlic salt**
- 1 **teaspoon dried thyme**
- 1 **teaspoon dried oregano**
- 1/2 **teaspoon celery salt**
- 1/2 **teaspoon pepper**
- 2 **tablespoons butter, melted**

With a meat fork, pierce holes in both sides of steak. Place in a large resealable bag. Combine the onion, lemon juice, oil, garlic salt, thyme, oregano, celery salt and pepper; pour over meat. Cover and refrigerate for 6 hours or overnight.

Drain and discard marinade. Broil steak 6 in. from the heat for 8 minutes. Brush with butter and turn. Broil 6 minutes longer or until meat reaches desired doneness (for medium-rare, a meat thermometer should read 145°; medium, 160°; well-done, 170°). **Yield:** 10 servings.

Nutrition Facts: 1 serving equals 250 calories, 15 g fat (5 g saturated fat), 82 mg cholesterol, 335 mg sodium, 3 g carbohydrate, 1 g fiber, 26 g protein.

Steak Diane

Phoebe Carre, Mullica Hill, New Jersey

When I want to provide a memorable dinner for my family or guests but don't want to spend hours in the kitchen, this is the recipe I rely on. We relish the savory sauce poured over the steaks.

- 4 **beef rib eye steaks (1/2 inch thick and 8 ounces *each*)**
- 1/4 **teaspoon pepper**
- 1/8 **teaspoon salt**
- 2 **tablespoons finely chopped green onion**
- 1/2 **teaspoon ground mustard**
- 4 **tablespoons butter, *divided***
- 1 **tablespoon lemon juice**
- 1-1/2 **teaspoons Worcestershire sauce**
- 1 **tablespoon minced fresh parsley**
- 1 **tablespoon minced fresh chives**

Sprinkle steaks on both sides with pepper and salt. In a large skillet, cook onion and mustard in 2 tablespoons butter for 1 minute.

Add steaks; cook for 2-5 minutes on each side or until the meat reaches desired doneness (for medium-rare, a meat thermometer should read 145°; medium, 160°; well-done, 170°).

Remove steaks to a serving platter and keep warm. In the same skillet, add the lemon juice, Worcestershire sauce and remaining butter; cook and stir for 2 minutes or until thickened. Add parsley and chives. Serve with steaks. **Yield:** 4 servings.

Roast Beef with Gravy

Tracy Ashbeck, Wisconsin Rapids, Wisconsin

Start this simple roast in the morning and you'll have tender slices of meat and gravy ready at supper time. The flavorful beef is loaded with homemade taste and leaves plenty left over for main dishes later in the week.

- 1 **boneless beef sirloin tip roast (about 4 pounds)**
- 1/2 **cup all-purpose flour, *divided***
- 1 **envelope onion soup mix**
- 1 **envelope brown gravy mix**
- 2 **cups cold water**

Hot mashed potatoes

Cut roast in half; rub with 1/4 cup flour. Place in 5-qt. slow cooker. In a bowl, combine soup and gravy mixes and remaining flour; stir in water until blended. Pour over roast.

Cover and cook on low for 6-8 hours or until meat is tender. Slice roast; serve slices with mashed potatoes and gravy. **Yield:** 16 servings.

Broiled Sirloin

Mushroom Beef Tenderloin

Festive Beef Tenderloin

Leann Meeds, Klamath Falls, Oregon

Dressing up a tenderloin steak is unbelievably easy when you add this seasoned cracker crumb/herb topping.

- **4 beef tenderloin steaks (about 1-1/2 inches thick *each*)**
- **1/4 cup crushed saltines**
- **1/4 cup mayonnaise**
- **2 tablespoons minced fresh parsley**
- **2 teaspoons prepared horseradish**
- **1/4 teaspoon pepper**

Broil steaks 3-4 in. from the heat for 8 minutes on each side.

Combine the cracker crumbs, mayonnaise, parsley, horseradish and pepper. Spread over steaks.

Broil 2-6 minutes longer or until meat reaches desired doneness (for medium-rare, a meat thermometer should read 145°; medium, 160°; well-done, 170°). **Yield:** 4 servings.

Quick Tip

When crushing the saltines for Festive Beef Tenderloin, simply set the crackers in a resealable bag. Press out as much air as possible, seal the bag and use a rolling pin to crush the crackers.

Festive Beef Tenderloin

Fillet Mignon with Garlic Cheese Butter

Donna Mahoney, Milford, Connecticut

I'm always looking for new and exciting recipes to make. I think this one is a real winner.

- **1 large whole garlic bulb**
- **1/4 teaspoon olive oil**
- **3/4 teaspoon minced fresh thyme *or* 1/4 teaspoon dried thyme**
- **1/4 cup butter, softened**
- **4-1/2 teaspoons crumbled blue cheese**
- **2 beef tenderloin steaks (6 ounces *each*)**
- **1/2 teaspoon pepper**
- **2 bacon strips**

Remove papery outer skin from garlic (do not peel or separate cloves). Cut top off of garlic bulb. Brush with oil. Sprinkle with thyme. Wrap the bulb in heavy-duty foil. Bake at 425° for 30-35 minutes or until softened. Cool for 10-15 minutes. Squeeze garlic into a mini-food processor. Add butter; process until smooth. Transfer mixutre to a small bowl. Stir in cheese. Cover and refrigerate for at least 1 hour.

Rub both sides of steaks with pepper. Wrap a bacon strip around each steak; secure with a toothpick.

Broil 4-6 in. from the heat for 8-12 minutes on each side or until meat reaches desired doneness (for medium-rare a meat thermometer reads 145°; medium, 160°; well-done, 170°), basting with butter mixture. Serve with any remaining butter. **Yield:** 2 servings.

Mushroom Beef Tenderloin

Blanche Stevens, Anderson, Indiana

This quick-to-fix dish looks special and tastes delicious. A delightful mushroom sauce nicely complements the beef tenderloin. I like to serve it with toasted French bread.

- **3/4 pound fresh mushrooms, sliced**
- **5 tablespoons butter, *divided***
- **2 teaspoons all-purpose flour**
- **1 teaspoon salt**
- **1/4 teaspoon pepper**
- **1 cup heavy whipping cream**
- **1 tablespoon minced fresh parsley**
- **6 beef tenderloin steaks (1-1/2 inches thick and 4 ounces *each*)**

In a large skillet, saute mushrooms in 3 tablespoons butter for 6-8 minutes or until tender. Stir in the flour, salt and pepper until blended. Gradually add the cream. Bring to a gentle boil; cook and stir for 1-2 minutes or until thickened. Stir in parsley; set aside and keep warm.

Meanwhile, in another large skillet, heat the remaining butter over medium-high heat. Cook the steaks for 6-7 minutes on each side or until a meat reaches desired doneness (for medium-rare, a meat thermometer should read 145°; medium, 160°; well-done, 170°). Serve steaks with the mushroom sauce. **Yield:** 6 servings.

Artichoke Beef Steaks

Light green artichokes and vibrant pimientos make these colorful steaks, from our Test Kitchen, perfect for any special occasion. If weather permits, grill the steaks outside and prepare the topping in a skillet as directed. They're great with mashed potatoes and corn.

- 1 **jar (6-1/2 ounces) marinated artichoke hearts**
- 4 **boneless beef rib eye steaks (3/4 inch thick and about 8 ounces *each*)**
- 1/2 **teaspoon salt**
- 2 **tablespoons butter**
- 1 **small onion, sliced and separated into rings**
- 1 **garlic clove, minced**
- 1 **jar (2 ounces) sliced pimientos, drained**

Cheese-Stuffed Flank Steak

Cheese-Stuffed Flank Steak

Evelyn Moll, Tulsa, Oklahoma

This pretty rolled steak never fails to impress dinner guests. Chopped pecans add a delicious crunch to the cheesy stuffing, while rosemary and thyme subtly flavor the tender meat.

- 1 **beef flank steak (3/4 pound)**
- 1 **can (6 ounces) pineapple juice**
- 1 **tablespoon Worcestershire sauce**
- 1 **small onion, chopped**
- 1/2 **teaspoon dried thyme**
- 1/4 **teaspoon dried rosemary, crushed**
- 1/4 **teaspoon salt**
- 1/8 **teaspoon pepper**

STUFFING
- 1/2 **cup soft bread crumbs**
- 1/2 **cup shredded cheddar cheese**
- 2 **tablespoons chopped pecans**
- 4-1/2 **teaspoons finely chopped onion**
- 4-1/2 **teaspoons minced fresh parsley**
- 1/4 **teaspoon dried minced garlic**
- 1 **tablespoon vegetable oil**

Flatten steak to 1/4-in. thickness. In a bowl, combine the pineapple juice, Worcestershire sauce, onion, thyme, rosemary, salt and pepper.

Pour half of the marinade into a resealable plastic bag; add meat. Seal bag and turn to coat; refrigerate for 4-8 hours. Cover and refrigerate remaining pineapple juice mixture.

Drain and discard marinade from meat. For stuffing, in a bowl, combine the bread crumbs, cheese, pecans, onion, parsley and garlic. Sprinkle stuffing over meat. Roll up jelly-roll style, starting with a short side. Tie with kitchen string.

In a small skillet, brown meat in oil until browned on all sides. Pour reserved marinade into skillet. Bring to a boil. Reduce heat; cover and simmer for 30 minutes or until tender. Thicken pan juices if desired. **Yield:** 2 servings.

Drain artichokes, reserving 1 tablespoon marinade. Cut artichokes in half and set aside. Sprinkle steaks with salt.

In a large skillet, cook steaks over medium-high heat in butter for 4 minutes on each side or until the meat reaches desired doneness (for medium-rare, a meat thermometer should read 145°; medium, 160°; well-done, 170°). Remove to a serving platter; keep warm.

In same skillet, saute onion and garlic in reserved marinade for 3 minutes. Add artichokes and pimientos; heat through. Serve with steaks. **Yield:** 4 servings.

Artichoke Beef Steaks

Tender Beef Brisket

Tender Beef Brisket

Sondra Morrow, Mesa, Arizona

A touch of sugar mellows the flavorful sauce that's drizzled over this brisket. The original recipe came to me from a friend, but I revised it for the slow cooker. I love coming home to the pleasant aroma of this savory brisket.

- 1 fresh beef brisket (3 to 4 pounds), trimmed and cut in half
- 1 cup ketchup
- 1 small onion, chopped
- 2 tablespoons cider vinegar
- 1 tablespoon prepared horseradish
- 1 tablespoon prepared mustard
- 1 teaspoon sugar
- 1/2 teaspoon pepper

Place the brisket in a 3-qt. slow cooker. In a bowl, combine the remaining ingredients. Pour mixture over brisket. Cover and cook on low for 6 hours or until tender.

Remove the beef; set aside. Pour the sauce into a saucepan; cook, uncovered, over low heat for 13-15 minutes or until reduced and thickened, stirring occasionally. Slice the meat across the grain; serve with sauce. **Yield:** 6-8 servings.

Editor's Note: This is a fresh beef brisket, not corned beef. The meat comes from the first cut of the brisket.

Garlic 'n' Pepper Prime Rib

Debbie Konovitz, Tonawanda, New York

Family and friends are delighted to see this roast adorning our table at celebrations throughout the year. It's a fancy favorite that's actually fuss-free.

- 1 small end beef rib roast (about 4 pounds)

Coarsely ground pepper

- 1 large onion, chopped
- 4 to 5 garlic cloves, minced
- 1-1/2 cups beef broth
- 1/3 cup ketchup

Sprinkle roast with pepper; place rib side down in a small roasting pan. Combine onion and garlic; spread over all sides of roast. Combine broth and ketchup; spoon 3/4 cup over roast. Set remaining broth mixture aside.

Bake, uncovered, at 325° for 2 hours or until meat reaches desired doneness (for medium-rare, a meat thermometer should read 145°; medium, 160°; well-done, 170°). Baste with pan drippings every 20 minutes, adding reserved broth mixture as needed. Let stand for 10 minutes before slicing.

Stir any remaining broth mixture into pan drippings; heat through and serve with roast. **Yield:** 6-8 servings.

Lemon Rib Eyes

Bill Huntington, Port Orchard, Washington

We have these tempting steaks often at my house. The mouth-watering combination of lemon juice and tangy feta cheese makes this an easy way to dress up rib eyes.

- 1-1/2 teaspoons dried basil
- 1-1/2 teaspoons dried oregano
- 1 teaspoon garlic powder
- 1/2 teaspoon salt
- 1/8 teaspoon pepper
- 2 beef rib eye steaks (8 ounces *each*)
- 1 tablespoon olive oil
- 1 tablespoon lemon juice
- 2 tablespoons crumbled feta *or* blue cheese, optional
- 1 tablespoon sliced ripe olives, optional

Lemon slices, optional

Combine basil, oregano, garlic powder, salt and pepper; rub over steaks. In a skillet, cook steaks in oil for 11-15 minutes or until meat reaches desired doneness (for medium-rare, a meat thermometer should read 145°; medium, 160°; well done, 170°).

Transfer to a serving platter. Drizzle with lemon juice. If desired, top with cheese and olives and garnish with lemon. **Yield:** 2 servings.

Garlic 'n' Pepper Prime Rib

Bacon Swiss Meat Loaf

Kimberly Lund, Park City, Kansas

The mellow flavor of Swiss cheese and the sweet, smoky flavor of bacon make this meat loaf stand out from any other. Round out the meal with a side of homemade mashed potatoes.

> 1 **egg**
> 1/4 **cup evaporated milk**
> 1-1/2 **cups (6 ounces) shredded Swiss cheese,** *divided*
> 1 **cup crumbled cooked bacon (about 12 bacon strips),** *divided*
> 1/2 **cup soft bread crumbs**
> 1/2 **teaspoon garlic powder**
> 1/2 **teaspoon onion powder**
> 1-1/2 **pounds ground beef**

In a large bowl, combine the egg, milk, 1 cup Swiss cheese, 3/4 cup bacon, bread crumbs, garlic powder and onion powder. Crumble beef over mixture and mix well. Shape into a loaf in a greased 11-in. x 7-in. x 2-in. baking dish.

Bake, uncovered, at 350° for 1 hour or until meat is no longer pink and a meat thermometer reads 160°. Drain. Sprinkle with remaining cheese and bacon. Bake 3-5 minutes longer or until cheese is melted. Let stand for 10 minutes before slicing. **Yield:** 6 servings.

Spinach-Stuffed Steak

Spinach-Stuffed Steak

Jetta Kaune, Ft. Huachuca, Arizona

A succulent mixture of spinach, peppers and sunflower kernels creates an extra-special filling for these steak slices. When I have time, I roast my own sweet peppers for the filling, but the jarred variety work just as well.

> 1 **package (10 ounces) frozen chopped spinach, thawed and drained**
> 1 **jar (7 ounces) roasted red peppers, drained**
> 1 **egg white**
> 1/2 **cup seasoned bread crumbs**
> 1/4 **cup grated Parmesan cheese**
> 1/4 **cup sunflower kernels, toasted**
> 1 **garlic clove, minced**
> 1/2 **teaspoon salt**
> 1 **beef flank steak (about 1-1/2 pounds)**

In a bowl, combine the first eight ingredients; mix well.

Cut steak horizontally from a long edge to within 1/2 in. of opposite edge; open (like a book) and flatten to 1/2-in. thickness. Spread spinach mixture over the steak to within 1 in. of edges. Roll up, jelly-roll style, starting with a long side; tie with kitchen string.

Place in a greased 13-in. x 9-in. x 2-in. baking dish. Cover and bake at 350° for 1 hour. Uncover; bake 30-45 minutes longer or until tender. Let stand for 10-15 minutes. Cut into 1/2-in. slices. **Yield:** 6 servings.

Bacon Swiss Meat Loaf

Quick Tip

To ease the job of slicing uncooked meat, partially freeze it first. When it's firm, you can cut the meat into uniform strips without much effort.

Surf 'n' Turf Tenderloin

Surf 'n' Turf Tenderloin

Colleen Gonring, Brookfield, Wisconsin

Indulge in this restaurant-style dish that combines the best of land and sea. Shrimp are stuffed inside thick, juicy tenderloins, then topped with a delicious onion-garlic sauce.

    1   tablespoon finely chopped onion
    1   garlic clove, minced
    2   tablespoons olive oil, *divided*
    2   tablespoons butter, *divided*
  1/4   cup beef broth
   16   uncooked medium shrimp
        (about 1/2 pound), peeled and
        deveined
    1   tablespoon minced fresh parsley
    4   beef tenderloin steaks (1-1/2 to 2
        inches thick and 6 ounces *each*)

In a small skillet, saute onion and garlic in 1 tablespoon oil and 1 tablespoon butter until tender. Add broth; cook and stir for 1 minute. Add the shrimp; cook and stir until shrimp turn pink, about 3-5 minutes. Add parsley.

Meanwhile, make a horizontal cut three-fourths of the way through each steak. Place three shrimp in each pocket. Cover remaining shrimp and sauce for garnish; set aside and keep warm.

In a large skillet, heat remaining oil and butter over medium-high heat. Add steaks; cook until meat reaches desired doneness (about 10-13 minutes for medium, 160°), turning once. Top with remaining shrimp and sauce. **Yield:** 4 servings.

Barbecued Short Ribs

Cheryl Niemela, Cokato, Minnesota

People like the blending of many different flavors in this recipe. I consider it a very special one and generally fix it for company. It always receives rave reviews.

    5   pounds bone-in beef short ribs,
        trimmed
    2   medium onions, finely chopped
    2   garlic cloves, minced
    2   tablespoons olive oil
    1   can (14-1/2 ounces) diced
        tomatoes, undrained
    1   cup chili sauce
  1/3   cup soy sauce
  1/3   cup honey
  1/4   cup packed brown sugar
  1/4   cup ketchup
    2   teaspoons chili powder
  1/2   teaspoon ground ginger
  1/8   teaspoon cayenne pepper
  1/8   teaspoon dried oregano
  1/8   teaspoon Liquid Smoke,
        optional

Place ribs in a Dutch oven; add water to cover by 2 in. Bring to a boil. Reduce heat; simmer, uncovered, for 1-1/2 to 2 hours or until tender.

Meanwhile, in a saucepan, saute onions and garlic in oil until tender. Add remaining ingredients; bring to a boil. Reduce heat; simmer, uncovered, for 30 minutes, stirring occasionally.

Drain ribs. Arrange on a broiler pan and baste with barbecue sauce. Broil 4 to 5 in. from the heat for 5-10 minutes on each side or until sauce is bubbly. **Yield:** 6-8 servings.

Cranberry Beef Brisket

Annette Bartle, Lees Summit, Missouri

My mother-in-law gave me the recipe for this tangy brisket that yields a lot. It is great to make on a Saturday or Sunday night so the leftover beef can be used in other recipes later in the workweek.

    1   beef brisket (4 to 5 pounds)
    2   tablespoons vegetable oil
    1   can (16 ounces) whole-berry
        cranberry sauce
  1/2   cup beef broth
  1/2   cup red wine *or* additional beef
        broth
    1   envelope onion soup mix

In a large skillet, brown beef in oil on both sides. Transfer to a greased roasting pan.

In a bowl, combine the remaining ingredients; pour over beef. Cover and bake at 350° for 3-4 hours or until meat is tender. Strain cooking juices if desired to serve with meat. **Yield:** 10-12 servings.

Editor's Note: This is a fresh beef brisket, not corned beef. The meat comes from the first cut of the brisket.

Barbecued Short Ribs

Meatballs Sausage Dinner (p. 2

Chapter 2

One-Dish Dinners

Meat and potatoes taste best when served together in the same dish. That's why we assembled this chapter featuring homemade meat pies, simmering stews, comforting casseroles and other meal-in-one wonders.

Chili Beef Bake

Martha Huffman, Monticello, Arkansas

We served this zesty casserole at a fund-raising luncheon for a local college. The students went crazy for it and came back for seconds and thirds. Some students even asked for the recipe, which relies on convenient canned beans, soups and tomatoes.

2   pounds ground beef
1   medium onion, chopped
1   garlic clove, minced
1   teaspoon chili powder
1   teaspoon salt
1/4 teaspoon pepper
12 flour tortillas (6 inches)
2   cans (15 ounces *each*) pinto beans, rinsed and drained
6   slices process American cheese
2   cans (10-3/4 ounces *each*) condensed cream of chicken soup, undiluted
1   can (10 ounces) diced tomatoes and green chilies, undrained

In a skillet, brown beef; drain. Add onion and garlic; cook until tender. Remove form the heat; add chili powder, salt and pepper.

Place six tortillas in a greased 13-in. x 9-in. x 2-in. baking dish, overlapping slightly. Top with half of the meat mixture. Layer with beans, remaining meat mixture, cheese and remaining tortillas. Combine soup and tomatoes; pour over tortillas (dish will be full). Bake, uncovered, at 350° for 30 minutes or until bubbly and heated through. **Yield:** 8 servings.

Stovetop Hamburger Casserole

Stovetop Hamburger Casserole

Edith Landinger, Longview, Texas

This is quick comfort food at its best. It's hearty and mildly seasoned, so it's great for a fast supper that everyone in the family will enjoy.

1   package (7 ounces) small pasta shells
1-1/2 pounds ground beef
1   large onion, chopped
3   medium carrots, chopped
1   celery rib, chopped
3   garlic cloves, minced
3   cups cubed cooked red potatoes
1   can (15-1/4 ounces) whole kernel corn, drained
2   cans (8 ounces *each*) tomato sauce
1-1/2 teaspoons salt
1/2 teaspoon pepper
1   cup (4 ounces) shredded cheddar cheese

Cook pasta shells according to package directions. Meanwhile, in a large skillet, cook beef and onion over medium heat until meat is no longer pink; drain.

Add the carrots, celery and garlic; cook and stir for 5 minutes or until vegetables are crisp-tender. Stir in the potatoes, corn, tomato sauce, salt and pepper; heat through.

Drain pasta shells and add to skillet; toss to coat. Sprinkle with cheddar cheese. Cover and cook until cheese is melted. **Yield:** 6 servings.

Hungry Man's Dinner

Sharon Howard, Gum Spring, Virginia

This recipe from my mother is one I grew up with. As the name implies, it's a casserole that will satisfy the biggest of appetites.

1-1/2 pounds ground beef
2   celery ribs, sliced
1   medium onion, chopped
1/2 cup chopped green pepper
1   garlic clove, minced
1   can (16 ounces) pork and beans
1   can (15 ounces) garbanzo beans *or* chickpeas, undrained
1   can (6 ounces) tomato paste
3/4 cup water
1   teaspoon salt
1   teaspoon paprika

In a skillet, cook beef, celery, onion, green pepper and garlic over medium heat until the meat is no longer pink and vegetables are tender. Stir in the remaining ingredients. Simmer, uncovered, for 30 minutes or until heated through. **Yield:** 6-8 servings.

Quick Tip

If aluminum foil gives you trouble when transporting casseroles, you might give this trick a try. Instead, put the casserole dish inside a clear plastic oven bag. The bag traps any spills, doesn't melt and potluck organizers can see what's inside.

Savory Meat Pie

Paula L'Hirondelle, Red Deer, Alberta

A friend gave me this recipe after I had mentioned that my meat pies lacked "punch." The pie has a delicious, distinctive flavor thanks to lots of spices. Flecks of carrots peek out of each neat slice.

- 2 medium potatoes, peeled and quartered
- 1 pound ground beef
- 3/4 cup sliced green onions
- 1 large carrot, finely chopped
- 1 garlic clove, minced
- 1/2 teaspoon dried thyme
- 1/2 teaspoon rubbed sage
- 1/2 teaspoon salt
- 1/2 teaspoon pepper
- 1/4 teaspoon celery salt

Pinch ground cinnamon

- 1/4 cup minced fresh parsley
- 1/4 cup chili sauce

Pastry for double-crust pie (9 inches)

- 1 tablespoon Dijon mustard
- 1 tablespoon milk

In a saucepan, cook potatoes in boiling water until tender; mash and set aside. Meanwhile, in a skillet, brown the beef; drain. Stir in the next nine ingredients. Simmer for 4-5 minutes. Stir in the potatoes, parsley and chili sauce; remove from heat.

Place bottom pastry in a 9-in. pie plate; brush with mustard. Add the meat mixture. Top the meat mixture with remaining pastry; seal and flute edges. Cut slits in the top crust.

Brush top crust with milk. Bake at 450° for 10 minutes. Reduce heat to 350°; bake 25 minutes longer or until golden brown. **Yield:** 6 servings.

Potato Beef Casserole

Shirley Goering, New Ulm, Minnesota

I sometimes add chopped onion when browning the ground beef for this fast-to-fix main dish. I often serve it for dinner or double the recipe to take to potlucks where it's always a hit.

- 4 medium potatoes, peeled and sliced
- 1 pound ground beef, cooked and drained
- 1 can (10-3/4 ounces) condensed cream of chicken soup, undiluted
- 1 can (10-1/2 ounces) condensed vegetable beef soup, undiluted
- 1/2 teaspoon salt

In a large bowl, combine all ingredients. Transfer mixture to a greased 2-qt. baking dish. Cover and bake casserole at 350° for 1-1/2 hours or until the potatoes are tender. **Yield:** 4-6 servings.

Tater Taco Casserole

Tater Taco Casserole

Ronna Lewis, Plains, Kansas

Our family lives and works on a ranch. I like to prepare this flavorful main dish ahead of time and freeze it for later use. Round out your meal by serving it with a tossed salad or nacho chips and dip.

- 2 pounds ground beef
- 1/4 cup chopped onion
- 1 envelope taco seasoning
- 2/3 cup water
- 1 can (11 ounces) whole kernel corn, drained
- 1 can (11 ounces) condensed fiesta nacho cheese soup, undiluted
- 1 package (32 ounces) frozen Tater Tots

In a skillet, cook beef and onion over medium heat until meat is no longer pink; drain. Stir in taco seasoning and water. Simmer, uncovered, for 5 minutes. Add corn and soup; mix well.

Transfer to a greased 13-in. x 9-in. x 2-in. baking dish. Arrange Tater Tots in a single layer over the top. Bake, uncovered, at 350° for 30-35 minutes or until potatoes are crispy and golden brown. **Yield:** 8 servings.

Savory Meat Pie

Quick Tip

Give your meat pies a tasty twist. After forming the crust, line it with slices of process Swiss cheese. Then, top the filling with another layer of cheese slices before adding the top crust.

Taco Potato Pie

Taco Potato Pie

Betty Jorsvick, Olds, Alberta

I made several of these hearty pies for a branding bee on our cattle ranch. Everybody had to have the recipe. With mashed potatoes, ground beef, beans and fresh vegetables, it's truly a meal in itself.

> 2 **cups cold mashed potatoes (prepared with milk and butter)**
> 1 **envelope taco seasoning, *divided***
> 1 **pound ground beef**
> 1/2 **cup chopped onion**
> 1 **can (16 ounces) refried beans**
> 1/2 **cup barbecue sauce**
> 1/4 **cup water**
> 1 **cup shredded lettuce**
> 1 **medium tomato, seeded and chopped**
> 1 **cup (4 ounces) shredded cheddar cheese**

Sour cream

Combine the potatoes and 2 tablespoons taco seasoning. Press into a greased 9-in. deep-dish pie plate; set aside.

In a skillet, cook beef and onion over medium heat until meat is no longer pink; drain. Stir in the beans, barbecue sauce, water and remaining taco seasoning. Cook and stir until hot and bubbly. Spoon into potato crust.

Bake at 350° for 30-35 minutes or until heated through. Top with lettuce, tomato, cheese and sour cream. **Yield:** 4-6 servings.

Meatball Potato Supper

Sonya Morton, Molena, Georgia

I'm frequently asked to bring this savory dish to potluck dinners. Folks must enjoy it, because there is never any extra to bring home!

> 2 **eggs**
> 1/2 **cup dry bread crumbs**
> 1 **envelope onion soup mix**
> 1-1/2 **pounds lean ground beef**
> 2 **tablespoons all-purpose flour**
> 6 **medium potatoes, peeled and thinly sliced**
> 1 **can (10-3/4 ounces) condensed cream of celery soup, undiluted**
> 1 **cup milk**

Paprika, optional

In a bowl, combine the eggs, bread crumbs and soup mix. Crumble beef over mixture and mix well. Shape into 1-in. balls. In a large skillet, brown meatballs in small batches over medium heat; drain. Sprinkle with flour; gently roll to coat.

Place half of the potatoes in a greased 2-1/2-qt. baking dish. Top with meatballs and remaining potatoes. In a bowl, combine soup and milk until blended; pour over potatoes. Sprinkle with paprika if desired. Cover and bake at 350° for 60-65 minutes or until the potatoes are tender. **Yield:** 6-8 servings.

Beef Veggie Casserole

Patti Keith, Ebensburg, Pennsylvania

This satisfying, stew-like casserole is a breeze to fix because it uses cooked roast beef, an envelope of gravy mix and convenient refrigerated buttermilk biscuits. Frozen veggies also make the meal a snap to prepare, but feel free to add the vegetables sitting in the fridge from last night's dinner instead.

> 1 **envelope mushroom gravy mix**
> 3/4 **cup water**
> 2 **cups cubed cooked beef**
> 2 **cups frozen mixed vegetables**
> 2 **medium potatoes, peeled, cubed and cooked**
> 1 **tube (12 ounces) refrigerated buttermilk biscuits, separated into 10 biscuits**

In a large saucepan, combine gravy mix and water until smooth. Bring to a boil; cook and stir for 1 minute or until thickened. Stir in the beef, vegetables and potatoes; heat through.

Transfer to a greased 8-in. square baking dish. Top with biscuits. Bake, uncovered, at 400° for 12-16 minutes or until bubbly and biscuits are golden brown. **Yield:** 5 servings.

Beef Veggie Casserole

Pork and Beef Barbecue

Corbin Detgen, Buchanan, Michigan

It's the combination of beef stew meat and pork tenderloin that keeps friends and family asking about these tangy sandwiches. Try topping them with lettuce and tomatoes for some extra variety.

✓ *Uses less fat, sugar or salt. Includes Nutrition Facts and Diabetic Exchanges.*

- 1 can (6 ounces) tomato paste
- 1/2 cup packed brown sugar
- 1/4 cup chili powder
- 1/4 cup cider vinegar
- 2 teaspoons Worcestershire sauce
- 1 teaspoon salt
- 1-1/2 pounds beef stew meat, cut into 3/4-inch cubes
- 1-1/2 pounds pork chop suey meat *or* pork tenderloin, cut into 3/4-inch cubes
- 3 medium green peppers, chopped
- 2 large onions, chopped
- 14 sandwich rolls, split
- Lettuce and tomatoes, optional

In a 5-qt. slow cooker, combine the first six ingredients. Stir in the beef, pork, green peppers and onions. Cover and cook on high for 6-8 hours or until the meat is tender.

Remove meat; cool slightly. Shred meat with two forks. Return meat to the slow cooker. Serve on rolls with lettuce and chopped tomatoes if desired. **Yield:** 14 servings.

Nutrition Facts: 1 serving (prepared with lean beef stew meat and pork tenderloin) equals 315 calories, 7 g fat (2 g saturated fat), 59 mg cholesterol, 596 mg sodium, 40 g carbohydrate, 3 g fiber, 25 g protein. **Diabetic Exchanges:** 2-1/2 starch, 2 lean meat, 1 vegetable.

Sweet-Sour Beef

Oven Beef Hash

Dorothy Pritchett, Wills Point, Texas

With just the two of us, we usually have leftovers of some sort, so hash is a regular menu item at our house. It's nice to have one version that I can pop in the oven.

- 3 cups diced cooked potatoes
- 1-1/2 cups cubed cooked roast beef
- 1 can (5 ounces) evaporated milk
- 1/4 cup minced fresh parsley
- 1/4 cup finely chopped onion
- 2 teaspoons Worcestershire sauce
- 1/2 teaspoon salt
- 1/8 teaspoon pepper
- 1/3 cup crushed saltines
- 1 tablespoon butter, melted

In a large bowl, combine the first eight ingredients. Spoon mixture into a greased 1-1/2-qt. baking dish. Combine the saltines and butter; sprinkle over top. Bake, uncovered, at 350° for 30 minutes or until heated through. **Yield:** 4 servings.

Sweet-Sour Beef

Beth Husband, Billings, Montana

Pasta lovers will enjoy this sweet-and-sour specialty over noodles. Chock-full of tender beef, sliced carrots, green pepper and onion, it is a hit served over rice, too.

- 2 pounds boneless beef round *or* chuck steak, cut into 1-inch cubes
- 2 tablespoons vegetable oil
- 2 cans (8 ounces *each*) tomato sauce
- 2 cups sliced carrots
- 2 cups pearl onions
- 1 large green pepper, cut into 1-inch pieces
- 1/2 cup molasses
- 1/3 cup cider vinegar
- 1/4 cup sugar
- 2 teaspoons chili powder
- 2 teaspoons paprika
- 1 teaspoon salt
- Shell macaroni and snipped chives, optional

In a large skillet, brown steak in oil; transfer to a 5-qt. slow cooker. Add the next 10 ingredients; stir well. Cover and cook on low for 7-8 hours or until meat is tender. Thicken if desired. Serve over macaroni and garnish with chives if desired. **Yield:** 10-12 servings.

Quick Tip

Easily perk up the flavor of hash made from leftover roast and potatoes by adding a simple teaspoon or two of vinegar during the last five minutes of cooking.

For biscuits, combine flour, baking powder, celery salt, paprika, salt and pepper in a mixing bowl. Cut in butter until mixture resembles coarse meal. Add milk and stir until a soft dough forms. Drop by tablespoonfuls onto meat mixture.

Bake, uncovered, at 475° for 20 minutes or until biscuits are golden. **Yield:** 4 servings.

Meatballs Sausage Dinner

Meatballs Sausage Dinner

Elizabeth Martz, Pleasant Gap, Pennsylvania

One day I was having trouble deciding what to make for dinner. So I combined whatever was in the refrigerator and freezer! To my surprise, everyone loved this satisfying entree made complete with broccoli, potatoes, smoked kielbasa and ground beef.

- 1 **package (10 ounces) frozen chopped broccoli, thawed**
- 2 **medium potatoes, peeled and cubed**
- 3 **medium carrots, sliced**
- 1 **medium onion, chopped**
- 1 **pound smoked kielbasa *or* Polish sausage, halved and cut into 1-inch pieces**
- 1/2 **pound lean ground beef**
- 1 **can (14-1/2 ounces) beef broth**

Lemon-pepper seasoning to taste

In a large bowl, combine the first four ingredients. Transfer to a greased 13-in. x 9-in. x 2-in. baking pan. Sprinkle with sausage.

Shape beef into 1-in. balls; arrange over top. Pour broth over the casserole. Sprinkle with lemon-pepper. Bake casserole, uncovered, at 350° for 1 hour or until the meatballs are no longer pink. **Yield:** 6-8 servings.

Potato-Topped Casserole

Cheryl Buker, Eagle, Colorado

My family enjoys this basic, comforting casserole because it features their favorite ingredients. I sometimes stir in sliced black olives.

- 2 **pounds ground beef**
- 2 **cans (8 ounces *each*) tomato sauce**
- 1 **cup sliced fresh mushrooms, optional**
- 2 **garlic cloves, minced**

Salt and pepper to taste

- 4 **cups hot mashed potatoes (prepared with milk and butter)**
- 2 **cups (8 ounces) shredded cheddar cheese**

In a large skillet, cook beef over medium heat until no longer pink; drain. Stir in the tomato sauce, mushrooms if desired, garlic, salt and pepper.

Transfer to a greased 13-in. x 9-in. x 2-in. baking dish. Top with potatoes; sprinkle with cheese. Bake, uncovered, at 350° for 35-40 minutes or until heated through and cheese is melted. **Yield:** 8-10 servings.

Upside-Down Meat Pie

Cora Dowling, Toledo, Ohio

This recipe, which my sister gave me more than 30 years ago, is perfect whenever friends drop by—it mixes up in a jiffy, yet it's substantial and filling.

- 1 **pound ground beef**
- 1/2 **cup chopped onion**
- 1/2 **teaspoon salt**
- 1 **can (15 ounces) tomato sauce**

BAKING POWDER BISCUITS

- 1 **cup all-purpose flour**
- 2 **teaspoons baking powder**
- 1 **teaspoon celery salt**
- 1 **teaspoon paprika**
- 1/2 **teaspoon salt**
- 1/4 **teaspoon pepper**
- 3 **tablespoons butter**
- 1/2 **cup milk**

In a large skillet, cook ground beef and onion until the beef is browned and onion is tender; drain. Add salt and tomato sauce; simmer 10-15 minutes. Spoon mixture into a 2-qt. casserole; set aside.

Quick Tip

Prepare a brownie mix and then pop it into the oven when the Meatballs Sausage Dinner is done...dessert will be baking while you're eating. Serve the brownies with vanilla ice cream.

Cheesy Potato Beef Bake

Nicole Rute, Fall River, Wisconsin

I created this layered meat-and-potatoes casserole a few years ago. My family thinks it tastes great and I hope you will, too.

- **1 pound ground beef**
- **2 cans (4 ounces *each*) mushroom stems and pieces, drained, optional**
- **2 packages (5-1/4 ounces *each*) au gratin potatoes**
- **4 cups boiling water**
- **1-1/3 cups milk**
- **2 teaspoons butter**
- **1 teaspoon salt**
- **1/2 teaspoon seasoned salt**
- **1/2 teaspoon pepper**
- **1 cup (4 ounces) shredded cheddar cheese**

Cheesy Potato Beef Bake

In a skillet over medium heat, cook beef until no longer pink; drain. Place beef in a greased 13-in. x 9-in. x 2-in. baking pan. Top with mushrooms.

Combine potatoes and contents of sauce mix packets, water, milk, butter, salt, seasoned salt and pepper. Pour over beef and mushrooms. Cover and bake at 400° for 30 minutes or until heated through.

Sprinkle with cheese. Bake, uncovered, for 5 minutes or until cheese is melted. Let stand 10 minutes before serving. **Yield:** 8 servings.

Skillet Shepherd's Pie

Tirzah Sandt, San Diego, California

This meal-in-one is so hearty and delicious. It's easy to assemble with ground beef, veggies and savory mashed potatoes, so dinner is on the table in no time.

- **1 pound ground beef**
- **1 cup chopped onion**
- **2 cups frozen corn, thawed**
- **2 cups frozen peas, thawed**
- **2 tablespoons ketchup**
- **1 tablespoon Worcestershire sauce**
- **2 teaspoons minced garlic**
- **1 teaspoon beef bouillon granules**
- **1/2 cup boiling water**
- **1 tablespoon cornstarch**
- **1/2 cup sour cream**
- **3-1/2 cups mashed potatoes (prepared with milk and butter)**
- **3/4 cup shredded cheddar cheese**

In a large skillet, cook the beef and onion over medium heat until the meat is no longer pink; drain. Stir in the corn, peas, ketchup, Worcestershire sauce and garlic. Reduce heat; cover and simmer for 5 minutes.

Meanwhile, in a small bowl, dissolve bouillon in boiling water. Combine cornstarch and sour cream until smooth; stir into beef mixture until blended. Add bouillon mixture. Bring to a boil. Reduce heat, cook and stir until thickened.

Spread mashed potatoes over the top; sprinkle with cheese. Cover and cook until potatoes are heated through and cheese is melted. **Yield:** 6 servings.

Skillet Shepherd's Pie

Ham N Swiss-Topped Potatoes

Ham N Swiss-Topped Potatoes

Jill Hayes, Westerville, Ohio

This is one of husband's favorite recipes. I often double the sauce to make sure I have some left over. It can be reheated to put over a microwaved potato for a quick lunch.

    3 **medium baking potatoes
       (12 ounces** *each*)
    2 **tablespoons cornstarch**
    2 **cups milk**
    1 **tablespoon Dijon mustard**
  1/2 **teaspoon pepper**
  1/2 **cup shredded Swiss cheese**
    2 **cups cubed fully cooked lean
       ham**
    2 **cups steamed cut fresh
       asparagus**

Bake potatoes at 375° for 1 hour or until tender. Meanwhile, in a saucepan, combine the cornstarch and milk until smooth. Bring to a boil over medium heat; cook and stir for 2 minutes or until thickened.

Reduce heat; stir in the mustard, pepper and Swiss cheese. Cook and stir until the cheese is melted. Stir in ham and asparagus. Cook for 5 minutes or until heated through.

Cut potatoes in half lengthwise; place cut side up and fluff the pulp with a fork. Spoon 2/3 cup sauce over each half. **Yield:** 6 servings.

Mashed Potato Hot Dish

Tanya Abernathy, Yacolt, Washington

My cousin gave me this simple but savory recipe. Whenever I'm making homemade mashed potatoes, I throw in a few extra spuds so I can make this dish for supper the next night.

    1 **pound ground beef**
    1 **can (10-3/4 ounces) condensed
       cream of chicken soup,
       undiluted**
    2 **cups frozen French-style green
       beans**
    2 **cups hot mashed potatoes
       (prepared with milk and butter)**
  1/2 **cup shredded cheddar cheese**

In a large skillet, cook beef over medium heat until no longer pink; drain. Stir in soup and beans.

Transfer to a greased 2-qt. baking dish. Top with mashed potatoes; sprinkle with cheese. Bake, uncovered, at 350° for 20-25 minutes or until bubbly and cheese is melted. **Yield:** 4 servings.

Potato Corn Casserole

Elsie Dahl, Tower, Minnesota

According to my husband, potatoes are the best food there is! He loves them in a variety of dishes. This comforting casserole is quickly prepared in the microwave.

    1 **pound lean ground beef**
Salt and pepper to taste
  1/4 **cup diced onion**
    4 **medium potatoes, peeled and
       diced**
    1 **can (14-3/4 ounces) cream-style
       corn**
    1 **tablespoon butter**

Crumble ground beef into a shallow 2-qt. microwave-safe dish. Sprinkle with salt and pepper. Layer with onion, potatoes and corn. Dot with butter. Cover and microwave on high for 9-10 minutes; stir.

Cover and heat 7-9 minutes longer or until meat is no longer pink and the potatoes are tender. **Yield:** 4 servings.

Editor's Note: This recipe was tested in a 1,100-watt microwave.

Mashed Potato Hot Dish

Slow Cooker Beef Stew

Corned Beef Casserole

Jeri Butters, Englewood, Florida

This recipe has been a winner in our family for more than 50 years. My kids still request it when they come to visit, and it was one of the first recipes they called long distance to ask for after they got married.

- 1 **medium onion, chopped**
- 2 **tablespoons butter**
- 2 **tablespoons all-purpose flour**
- 1-1/2 **teaspoons salt**
- 1 **teaspoon Worcestershire sauce**
- 1/4 **teaspoon pepper**
- 2-1/2 **cups milk**
- 3 **medium potatoes, cooked and cubed**
- 1 **can (15-1/4 ounces) whole kernel corn, drained**
- 1 **can (12 ounces) corned beef**
- 1 **tube (12 ounces) refrigerated buttermilk biscuits**

In a large saucepan, cook onion in butter over medium heat until tender; remove from the heat. Stir in the flour, salt, Worcestershire sauce and pepper until blended. Gradually add the milk. Bring to a boil; cook and stir for 2 minutes or until thickened. Stir in the potatoes, corn and corned beef.

Transfer to a greased 13-in. x 9-in. x 2-in. baking dish. Bake, uncovered, at 400° for 30 minutes or until bubbly. Top with biscuits. Bake 10-15 minutes longer or until biscuits are golden brown. **Yield:** 8-10 servings.

Corned Beef Casserole

Slow Cooker Beef Stew

Earnestine Wilson, Waco, Texas

This is such an easy way to make a wonderful beef stew. Prepared in the slow cooker, the meat and vegetables turn out incredibly tender.

- 1-1/2 **pounds potatoes, peeled and cubed**
- 6 **medium carrots, cut into 1-inch slices**
- 1 **medium onion, coarsely chopped**
- 3 **celery ribs, coarsely chopped**
- 3 **tablespoons all-purpose flour**
- 1-1/2 **pounds beef stew meat, cut into 1-inch cubes**
- 3 **tablespoons vegetable oil**
- 1 **can (14-1/2 ounces) diced tomatoes, undrained**
- 1 **cup beef broth**
- 1 **teaspoon ground mustard**
- 1/2 **teaspoon salt**
- 1/2 **teaspoon pepper**
- 1/2 **teaspoon dried thyme**
- 1/2 **teaspoon browning sauce**

Layer the potatoes, carrots, onion and celery in a 5-qt. slow cooker. Place flour in a large resealable plastic bag. Add stew meat; seal and toss to coat evenly. In a large skillet, brown meat in oil in batches. Place over vegetables.

In a large bowl, combine the tomatoes, broth, mustard, salt, pepper, thyme and browning sauce. Pour over beef. Cover and cook on high for 1-1/2 hours. Reduce heat to low; cook 6-8 hours longer or until the meat and vegetables are tender. **Yield:** 8 servings.

Beefy Hash Brown Bake

Rochelle Boucher, Brooklyn, Wisconsin

A topping of french-fried onions provides a little crunch to this meaty main dish. Since this casserole is practically a meal in itself, I simply accompany it with a fresh fruit salad and a dessert.

- 4 **cups frozen shredded hash brown potatoes**
- 3 **tablespoons vegetable oil**
- 1/8 **teaspoon pepper**
- 1 **pound ground beef**
- 1 **cup water**
- 1 **envelope brown gravy mix**
- 1/2 **teaspoon garlic salt**
- 2 **cups frozen mixed vegetables**
- 1 **can (2.8 ounces) French-fried onions,** *divided*
- 1 **cup (4 ounces) shredded cheddar cheese,** *divided*

In a bowl, combine the potatoes, oil and pepper. Press into a greased 8-in. square baking dish. Bake, uncovered, at 350° for 15-20 minutes or until potatoes are thawed and set.

Meanwhile, in a saucepan, cook the beef over medium heat until no longer pink; drain. Stir in water, gravy mix and garlic salt. Bring to a boil; cook and stir for 2 minutes. Add vegetables; cook and stir for 5 minutes. Stir in half of the onions and cheese.

Pour over the potatoes. Bake for 5-10 minutes. Sprinkle top with the remaining onions and cheese; bake 5 minutes longer or until cheese is melted. **Yield:** 4 servings.

Hamburger Stew

Hamburger Stew
Julie Kretchman, Meyersdale, Pennsylvania

My grandmother gave me this recipe, so one taste of this flavorful stew always brings back warm memories of her.

- 1/2 **pound ground beef**
- 1/4 **cup chopped onion**
- 1/4 **cup chopped celery**
- 3/4 **cup beef broth**
- 1 **cup canned diced tomatoes with juice**
- 3/4 **cup cubed peeled potato**
- 1/4 **cup thinly sliced carrot**
- 2 **tablespoons uncooked long grain rice**
- 1/2 **teaspoon salt, optional**
- 1/8 **teaspoon pepper**

In a large saucepan, cook the beef, onion and celery over medium heat until meat is no longer pink; drain.

Stir in broth, tomatoes, potato, carrot, rice, salt if desired and pepper. Bring to a boil. Reduce heat; cover and simmer 40-45 minutes, until rice and vegetables are tender. **Yield:** 2 servings.

Deep-Dish Hunter's Pie
Christina Rulien, Marysville, Washington

My husband, an avid hunter, loves the seasoned garlic mashed potato topping on this hearty, meaty dish.

- 1-1/2 **pounds potatoes, peeled and cubed**
- 3 **garlic cloves, minced**
- 1/4 **cup milk**
- 1 **tablespoon butter**
- 1/4 **teaspoon dried rosemary, crushed**
- 1/2 **teaspoon salt**
- 1/8 **teaspoon pepper**

FILLING
- 1 **cup sliced fresh mushrooms**
- 1 **cup sliced carrots**
- 1/2 **cup chopped onion**
- 1/4 **cup chopped green pepper**
- 1 **tablespoon butter**
- 2 **cups cubed cooked venison**
- 1-1/2 **cups beef broth**
- 1/4 **teaspoon dried thyme**
- 1/8 **teaspoon ground nutmeg**
- 3 **tablespoons all-purpose flour**
- 3 **tablespoons cold water**
- 1/3 **cup shredded cheddar cheese**
- 2 **tablespoons minced parsley**

Cook potatoes in boiling water until tender; drain and mash. Add the garlic milk, butter, rosemary, salt and pepper set aside.

In a large skillet, saute mushrooms carrots, onion and green pepper in butter until tender. Add venison, broth thyme and nutmeg. Bring to a boil Reduce heat; cover and simmer for 25-30 minutes or until meat and vegetables are tender.

Combine the flour and water until smooth; stir into skillet. Bring to a boil cook and stir for 2 minutes or unti thickened. Transfer to a greased 2-qt baking dish.

Spread the mashed potatoes over the top. Bake, uncovered, at 350° for 30-40 minutes or until bubbly. Sprinkle top with cheese. Bake 5 minutes longer or until cheese is melted. Sprinkle with parsley. **Yield:** 6 servings.

Deep-Dish Hunter's Pie

Traditional Beef Potpie

Roll two-thirds of the dough into a 14-in. x 10-in. rectangle. Line the bottom and sides of an ungreased 11-in. x 7-in. baking dish. Roll remaining pastry into a 6-in. circle; cut into six wedges.

Spoon beef mixture into crust. Place pastry wedges on top. Bake, uncovered, at 450° for 10 minutes. Reduce heat to 350°; bake 30 minutes longer or until pastry is golden brown. **Yield:** 6 servings.

Bacon Potato Puff

DeEtta Rasmussen, Fort Madison, Iowa

Here's a delicious way to change up your mealtime routine. The golden brown puff is terrific on its own, or try it alongside scrambled eggs.

- 1/2 **pound sliced bacon, diced**
- 4 **eggs,** *separated*
- 1/4 **cup finely chopped onion**
- 1/2 **teaspoon ground mustard**
- 1/8 **teaspoon pepper**
- 2 **cups warm mashed potatoes (with added milk and butter)**
- 1/2 **cup shredded cheddar cheese**
- 1/4 **cup minced fresh parsley**

In a skillet, cook bacon until crisp; remove to paper towels to drain. Discard drippings. In a mixing bowl, beat egg yolks until light, about 2 minutes. Beat in onion, mustard and pepper. Place potatoes in a bowl; fold in egg yolk mixture. set aside 2 tablespoons bacon. Fold cheese, parsley and remaining bacon into potatoes. In a small mixing bowl, beat egg whites until stiff; fold into potato mixture.

Transfer to a greased 1-qt. baking dish. Sprinkle with reserved bacon. Bake, uncovered, at 325° for 45-50 minutes or until set and edges are golden brown. Serve immediately. **Yield:** 6-8 servings.

Traditional Beef Potpie

Beth Armstrong, Milwaukee, Wisconsin

Meal-in-one casseroles, like this recipe, are the perfect dinner solution on busy days. My family relies on this tasty pleaser often.

CRUST

- 1-1/2 **cups all-purpose flour**
- 2/3 **cup shredded cheddar cheese**
- 1/2 **teaspoon salt**
- 1/4 **teaspoon pepper**
- 1/8 **teaspoon dried thyme**
- 1/2 **cup shortening**
- 5 **to 6 tablespoons cold water**

FILLING

- 1-1/2 **pounds boneless beef round steak, cut into 1-inch cubes**
- 1 **medium onion, chopped**
- 1 **tablespoon vegetable oil**
- 1-1/2 **cups sliced fresh mushrooms**
- 2 **cups beef broth,** *divided*
- 3/4 **teaspoon salt**
- 1/2 **teaspoon dried thyme**
- 1/4 **teaspoon garlic powder**
- 1/8 **teaspoon pepper**
- 1-1/2 **cups cubed peeled potatoes**
- 1 **cup sliced carrots**
- 3/4 **cup sliced celery**
- 1/3 **cup all-purpose flour**
- 1/2 **teaspoon browning sauce, optional**

In a bowl, combine the flour, cheese, salt, pepper and thyme; cut in the shortening until mixture resembles coarse crumbs. Stir in the water just until moistened. Form dough into a ball. Cover and refrigerate.

Meanwhile, in a large saucepan or Dutch oven, brown beef and onion in oil. Add the mushrooms; saute mushrooms for 1 minute. Add 1 cup broth, salt, thyme, garlic powder and pepper; bring to a boil. Reduce heat; cover and simmer for 30 minutes.

Add the potatoes, carrots and celery; cover and simmer 20 minutes longer or until the meat is tender and vegetables are crisp-tender. Combine flour and remaining broth until smooth; gradually add to beef mixture. Bring to a boil; cook and stir for 2 minutes. Stir in browning sauce if desired. Reduce heat; keep warm.

Bacon Potato Puff

Meaty Macaroni Bake

In a skillet, cook beef and pork over medium heat until no longer pink; drain. Add the broth, potatoes, tomatoes, onion, ketchup, Worcestershire sauce, lemon juice and vinegar. Bring to a boil. Reduce heat; cover and simmer for 30 minutes.

Add the corn, hot pepper sauce, salt and pepper to meat and potato mixture. Simmer for 10 minutes, stirring occasionally. **Yield:** 6-8 servings.

Editor's Note: To remove kernels from cooked corncobs, stand one end of the cob on a cutting board. Run a sharp knife down the cob, cutting deeply to remove kernels. Lightly pack into freezer containers or plastic bags, leaving 1/2 inch headspace. Freeze for up to 10 months. Two medium ears yield about 1 cup kernels.

Meaty Macaroni Bake

Connie Helsing, Ashland, Nebraska

We go to lots of rodeos. This is an ideal casserole to make in the morning and pop into the oven when we return.

1-1/2	pounds ground beef
1	medium onion, chopped
1	garlic clove, minced
1	jar (14 ounces) spaghetti sauce
1	cup water
1	can (8 ounces) tomato sauce
1	can (6 ounces) tomato paste
1/2	teaspoon salt
1/8	teaspoon pepper
2	eggs, beaten
1/4	cup vegetable oil
1	package (7 ounces) elbow macaroni, cooked and drained
2	cans (4 ounces *each*) mushroom stems and pieces, drained
1	cup (4 ounces) shredded part-skim mozzarella cheese
1/4	cup grated Parmesan cheese
1	cup soft bread crumbs

Additional part-skim mozzarella cheese, optional

In a large skillet, cook the beef, onion and garlic over medium heat until meat is no longer pink; drain. Add the spaghetti sauce, water, tomato sauce, tomato paste, salt and pepper. Bring to a boil.

Reduce heat; simmer, uncovered, for 10 minutes.

In a bowl, combine the eggs, oil, macaroni, mushrooms, cheeses and bread crumbs. Spoon into a 3-qt. baking dish. Top with meat mixture. Bake, uncovered, at 350° for 30 minutes. Sprinkle with additional mozzarella cheese if desired. Let stand for 10 minutes before serving. **Yield:** 6-8 servings.

Meat 'n' Potato Stew

Mildred Sherrer, Fort Worth, Texas

My sons are real meat-and-potatoes men, so they request this recipe quite often. The addition of pork adds a tempting taste twist.

1	pound ground beef
1	pound boneless pork loin, cut into 1-inch cubes
1	can (14-1/2 ounces) beef broth
2	large potatoes, peeled and cut into 1-inch cubes
1	can (14-1/2 ounces) diced tomatoes, undrained
1	large onion, chopped
1/2	cup ketchup
1/4	cup Worcestershire sauce
1	tablespoon lemon juice
1	tablespoon white vinegar
1	cup whole kernel corn, drained

Hot pepper sauce to taste

Salt and pepper to taste

Orange-Flavored Beef and Potatoes

Paula Pelis Marchesi, New York, New York

This stick-to-your-ribs dish has never failed me. While it's baking, I can prepare a simple vegetable side dish, salad or dessert to complete the meal.

2	green onions, sliced
3	tablespoons soy sauce
2	tablespoons water
2	tablespoons white wine *or* additional water
1	tablespoon sugar
4	teaspoons vegetable oil, *divided*
1	tablespoon orange juice
1	teaspoon grated orange peel
1	teaspoon white vinegar
3/4	teaspoon ground ginger
1	tablespoon quick-cooking tapioca
1-1/2	pounds beef stew meat, cut into 1-inch cubes
1	pound small red potatoes, quartered

In a large bowl, combine the green onions, soy sauce, water, wine or additional water, sugar, 3 teaspoons oil, orange juice, peel, vinegar and ginger. Stir in tapioca and let stand for 15 minutes.

Place the beef and potatoes in a greased 11-in. x 7-in. x 2-in. baking dish. Pour tapioca mixture over the top. Cover and bake at 350° for 2 hours or until meat is tender. **Yield:** 6 servings.

Wild Rice-Stuffed Steaks

Ardith Baker, Beaverton, Oregon

Filled with a scrumptious, packaged rice mixture and seasoned with teriyaki sauce, these steaks are a favorite. Just four ingredients are required for the delightful entree, so it comes together in a snap.

- 1 **package (6.2 ounces) fast-cooking long grain and wild rice mix**
- 1/4 **cup chopped green onions**
- 6 **New York strip steaks (about 12 ounces *each*)**
- 1/2 **cup teriyaki sauce, *divided***

Cook rice according to package directions for microwave; cool. Stir in onions. Cut a pocket in each steak by slicing to within 1/2 in. of bottom. Stuff each with 1/4 cup rice mixture; secure with toothpicks. Brush steaks with 2 tablespoons teriyaki sauce.

Place on a broiler pan. Broil 4-6 in. from the heat for 4-6 minutes. Turn the steaks; brush with 2 tablespoons teriyaki sauce. Broil steaks 6-8 minutes longer or until meat reaches desired doneness (for medium-rare, a meat thermometer should read 145°; medium, 160°; well-done, 170°), basting frequently with the remaining sauce. Discard toothpicks. **Yield:** 6 servings.

Enchilada Casserole

Julie Huffman, New Lebanon, Ohio

This zippy Mexican casserole is a real winner at our house. It's so flavorful and filling, we usually just accompany it with rice and black beans. If your family has spicier tastes, increase the chili powder and use a medium or hot salsa.

- 1-1/2 **pounds ground beef**
- 1 **large onion, chopped**
- 1 **cup water**
- 2 **to 3 tablespoons chili powder**
- 1-1/2 **teaspoons salt**
- 1/2 **teaspoon pepper**
- 1/4 **teaspoon garlic powder**
- 2 **cups salsa, *divided***
- 10 **flour tortillas (8 inches), cut into 3/4-inch strips, *divided***
- 1 **cup (8 ounces) sour cream**
- 2 **cans (15-1/4 ounces *each*) whole kernel corn, drained**
- 4 **cups (16 ounces) shredded part-skim mozzarella cheese**

In a large skillet, cook beef and onion over medium heat until the meat is no longer pink; drain. Stir in the water, chili powder, salt, pepper and garlic powder. Bring to a boil. Reduce heat; simmer, uncovered, for 10 minutes.

Place 1/4 cup salsa each in two greased 8-in. square baking dishes.

Enchilada Casserole

Layer each dish with a fourth of the tortillas and 1/4 cup salsa.

Divide meat mixture, sour cream and corn between the two casseroles. Top with the remaining tortillas, salsa and cheese.

Cover and freeze one casserole for up to 1 month. Cover and bake second casserole at 350° for 35 minutes. Uncover; bake 5-10 minutes longer or until heated through.

To use frozen casserole: Thaw in the refrigerator for 24 hours. Remove from the refrigerator 30 minutes before baking. Bake as directed above. **Yield:** 2 casseroles (4-6 servings each).

Wild Rice-Stuffed Steaks

Quick Tip

Eliminate baked-on messes while reheating a serving of any cheese-topped dish with this handy tip. Stick a toothpick in the center of the serving, then "tent" a piece of paper towel over the top. You'll have very little splatter in your microwave and the cheese won't stick to the paper towel.

Meatball Stew

Chili-Stuffed Potatoes

Laura Perry, Exton, Pennsylvania

Microwave baked potatoes and canned chili make this filling dish a snap to take to the table! It's colorful, too, topped with fresh tomatoes, sour cream and shredded cheese. They're great for cookouts or picnic meals.

- 4 large baking potatoes (about 2 pounds)
- 1 can (15 ounces) vegetarian chili
- 1/2 cup shredded Mexican cheese blend
- 1 cup chopped seeded fresh tomatoes
- 1/4 cup sour cream
- 1/4 cup minced fresh cilantro *or* parsley

Scrub and pierce the potatoes; place on a microwave-safe plate. Microwave, uncovered, on high for 12-14 minutes or until tender, turning once.

Meanwhile, in a saucepan, heat chili. With a sharp knife, cut an "X" in each potato; fluff with a fork. Spoon chili over each potato; sprinkle with cheese. Top with tomatoes, sour cream and cilantro. **Yield:** 4 servings.

Editor's Note: This recipe was tested in a 1,100-watt microwave.

Meatball Stew

Iris Schultz, Miamisburg, Ohio

I came up with this hearty meal-in-one as another way to use frozen meatballs. It's quick to put together in the morning and ready when my husband gets home in the evening.

- 3 medium potatoes, peeled and cut into 1/2-inch cubes
- 1 package (16 ounces) fresh baby carrots, quartered
- 1 large onion, chopped
- 3 celery ribs, sliced
- 1 package (12 ounces) frozen fully cooked meatballs
- 1 can (10-3/4 ounces) condensed tomato soup, undiluted
- 1 can (10-1/2 ounces) beef gravy
- 1 cup water
- 1 envelope onion soup mix
- 2 teaspoons beef bouillon granules

Place potatoes, carrots, onion, celery and meatballs in a 5-qt. slow cooker.

In a bowl, combine the remaining ingredients. Pour over meatball mixture. Cover and cook on low for 9-10 hours or until the vegetables are crisp-tender. **Yield:** 6 servings.

Beef Stuffing Bake

Denise Goedeken, Platte Center, Nebraska

I work full-time, so I'm always looking for swift dishes that taste good. This one includes two of my kids' favorite foods—ground beef and stuffing. It goes over great at potluck suppers.

- 1 pound ground beef
- 1 small onion, chopped
- 1 package (10 ounces) beef- *or* pork-flavored stuffing mix
- 1 can (10-3/4 ounces) condensed cream of celery soup, undiluted
- 1 can (10-3/4 ounces) condensed cream of mushroom soup, undiluted
- 1 jar (4-1/2 ounces) sliced mushrooms, drained
- 1 cup water
- 1 cup frozen mixed vegetables

In a skillet, cook beef and onion over medium heat until meat is no longer pink; drain. Transfer to an ungreased 13-in. x 9-in. x 2-in. baking dish.

In a bowl, combine contents of stuffing seasoning packet, soups, mushrooms, water and vegetables. Sprinkle stuffing over beef mixture; top with soup mixture. Bake, uncovered, at 350° for 30 minutes or until heated through. **Yield:** 6-8 servings.

Chili-Stuffed Potatoes

Pepper Steak with Potatoes

Pepper Steak with Potatoes

Kristine Marra, Clifton Park, New York

I added potatoes to one of my beef dinner recipes to create this well-rounded skillet dish. It's a cinch to prepare because the potatoes are cooked in the microwave, plus it's satisfying enough for all the men in our house.

- **5 medium red potatoes, cut into 1/4-inch slices**
- **1/2 cup water**
- **1 pound boneless beef sirloin steak, thinly sliced**
- **1 garlic clove, minced**
- **2 tablespoons olive oil**
- **1 medium green pepper, julienned**
- **1 small onion, chopped**
- **Pepper to taste**
- **4 teaspoons cornstarch**
- **1 cup beef broth**

Place the potatoes and water in a microwave-safe bowl; cover and microwave on high for 5-7 minutes or until tender.

Meanwhile, in a large skillet, saute beef and garlic in oil until meat is no longer pink. Remove and keep warm; drain drippings. In the same skillet, saute the green pepper and onion until crisp-tender. Return beef to the pan. Add potatoes and pepper; heat through.

In a small saucepan, combine cornstarch and broth until smooth. Bring to a boil; cook and stir for 2 minutes or until thickened. Drizzle over meat mixture; toss to coat. **Yield:** 6 servings.

Editor's Note: This recipe was tested in a 1,100-watt microwave.

Corned Beef Potato Dinner

Brooke Staley, Mary Esther, Florida

For St. Patrick's Day, I usually prepare this dish instead of the traditional corned beef dinner. This takes less time because it makes good use of the microwave…and it's very tasty.

- **1 pound red potatoes, cut into small wedges**
- **1-1/2 cups water**
- **1 large onion, thinly sliced and separated into rings**
- **4 cups coleslaw mix**
- **8 ounces thinly sliced deli corned beef, cut into 1/4-inch strips**
- **1 tablespoon vegetable oil**
- **1/3 cup red wine vinegar**
- **4 teaspoons spicy brown mustard**
- **1 teaspoon sugar**
- **1 teaspoon caraway seeds**
- **1/2 teaspoon garlic powder**
- **1/2 teaspoon salt**
- **1/2 teaspoon pepper**

Place potatoes and water in a 3-qt. microwave-safe bowl. Cover; microwave on high for 4-5 minutes or until potatoes are crisp-tender. Add the onion; cover and cook for 1-2 minutes or until onions are tender. Stir in the coleslaw mix. Cover and cook for 2-3 minutes longer or until potatoes are tender; drain.

In a large skillet, saute corned beef in oil for 3-4 minutes; drain. Stir in the remaining ingredients. Cook and stir for 1 minute or until heated through. Add to the potato mixture; toss to combine. Cover and microwave for 1-2 minutes or until heated through. **Yield:** 4 servings.

Editor's Note: This recipe was tested in a 1,100-watt microwave.

Crescent Cheeseburger Pie

Carolyn Hayes, Marion, Illinois

I grab this recipe when I'm looking for an easy dinner that everyone will enjoy. Add a side salad, and presto, the meal is done!

- **1 pound ground beef**
- **1 small onion, chopped**
- **1 can (8 ounces) tomato sauce**
- **1/3 cup ketchup**
- **1/2 teaspoon salt**
- **1/4 teaspoon pepper**
- **5 to 6 slices process cheese (Velveeta)**
- **1 tube (8 ounces) refrigerated crescent rolls**

In a skillet, cook the beef and onion over medium heat until the meat is no longer pink; drain. Stir in tomato sauce, ketchup, salt and pepper; heat through. Spoon into an ungreased 9-in. pie plate. Arrange the cheese on top.

Bake at 400° for 2-3 minutes or until cheese begins to warm. Unroll crescent roll dough and separate into triangles. Place over cheese, pressing down on edges of pie plate to seal. Bake 10-12 minutes longer or until golden brown. Let stand for 5 minutes before cutting. **Yield:** 8 servings.

Corned Beef Potato Dinner

Hash Brown Beef Pie

Mina Dyck, Boissevain, Manitoba

Convenient frozen hash browns and shredded cheddar cheese top this hearty mixture of vegetables and ground beef. It has just the right combination of spices. Because I'm cooking for one, I like that the leftovers reheat well in the microwave.

- 1   pound ground beef
- 1   medium onion, chopped
- 1   garlic clove, minced
- 1   can (14-1/2 ounces) diced tomatoes, drained
- 1   teaspoon chili powder
- 1   teaspoon dried oregano
- 1/2 teaspoon salt
- 1/4 teaspoon pepper
- 1-1/2 cups frozen mixed vegetables

TOPPING
- 3   cups frozen shredded hash brown potatoes, thawed and drained
- 1   cup (8 ounces) shredded cheddar cheese
- 1   egg
- 1/8 teaspoon salt
- 1/8 teaspoon pepper

In a large skillet, cook beef, onion and garlic until beef is no longer pink; drain. Stir in tomatoes, chili powder, oregano, salt and pepper; bring to a boil. Reduce heat; simmer, uncovered, for 10 minutes. Stir in the vegetables.

Pour into a greased 9-in. pie plate. Combine topping ingredients; spoon evenly over the meat mixture. Bake, uncovered, at 400° for 30 minutes. **Yield:** 6-8 servings.

Hash Brown Beef Pie

Meat Lover's Pizza Bake

Meat Lover's Pizza Bake

Carol Oakes, Sturgis, Michigan

I'm happy to share the recipe for this yummy pizza casserole. With ground beef and pepperoni, it's very satisfying. Instead of a typical pizza crust, it features a crust-like topping that's a snap to make with biscuit mix.

- 1   pound ground beef
- 1/2 cup chopped green pepper
- 1   can (15 ounces) pizza sauce
- 1   package (3-1/2 ounces) sliced pepperoni, chopped
- 1   can (2-1/4 ounces) sliced ripe olives, drained
- 2   cups (8 ounces) shredded part-skim mozzarella cheese
- 3/4 cup biscuit/baking mix
- 2   eggs
- 3/4 cup milk

In a large skillet, cook beef and green pepper over medium heat until meat is no longer pink; drain. Stir in the pizza sauce, pepperoni and olives. Transfer to a greased 11-in. x 7-in. x 2-in. baking dish. Sprinkle with cheese.

In a small bowl, combine the biscuit mix, eggs and milk until blended. Pour evenly over cheese. Bake, uncovered, at 400° for 25-30 minutes or until golden brown. Let stand for 10 minutes before serving. **Yield:** 6 servings.

Beefy Kraut and Rice

Kristi Baker, Sioux City, Iowa

My husband and I are both police officers, and after a long workday, I rely on meals that come together easily. This tasty hot dish is easy to make and has a tangy twist that even our kids enjoy.

- 1   pound ground beef
- 1   can (14 ounces) sauerkraut, rinsed and drained
- 1-1/2 cups water
- 1   can (10-3/4 ounces) condensed cream of mushroom soup, undiluted
- 1   cup uncooked long grain rice
- 1   envelope beefy mushroom soup mix
- 1/2 cup shredded Swiss cheese, optional

In a large skillet, cook beef over medium heat until no longer pink; drain. In a bowl, combine the beef, sauerkraut, water, soup, rice and soup mix.

Transfer to a greased 2-qt. baking dish. Cover and bake at 350° for 50-60 minutes or until rice is tender. Sprinkle top with Swiss cheese if desired. Bake for 5 minutes longer or until the cheese is melted. **Yield:** 4-6 servings.

Biscuit-Topped Beef N Beans

Eleanor McQuiston, Harrisville, Pennsylvania

I entered this recipe for the annual cookbook put out by our local newspaper and was thrilled to win a prize! I shared my winnings with the dear friend who gave the recipe to me.

- 1 pound ground beef
- 1/4 cup chopped green pepper
- 1 can (16 ounces) kidney beans, rinsed and drained
- 1 cup spaghetti sauce
- 1 can (4 ounces) mushroom stems and pieces, drained
- 1 tablespoon onion soup mix
- 1/4 teaspoon garlic powder
- 1 block (4 ounces) cheddar cheese, cut into 1/2-inch cubes
- 1 tube (12 ounces) refrigerated buttermilk biscuits
- 1 tablespoon butter, melted

In a skillet, cook beef and green pepper over medium heat until meat is no longer pink; drain. Stir in the beans, spaghetti sauce, mushrooms, soup mix and garlic powder; mix well. Bring to a boil.

Meanwhile, place a cheese cube in the center of each biscuit. Fold dough over cheese to cover; pinch to seal.

Transfer hot meat mixture to a greased 2-qt. baking dish. Place the biscuits seam side down over the beef mixture. Brush biscuits with butter. Bake, uncovered, at 400° for 18-20 minutes or until the biscuits are golden brown. **Yield:** 5 servings.

Two-Meat Macaroni

Terri Linn Griffin, Eugene, Oregon

Although I don't know the origin of this recipe, I do know my mother has pleased family and friends with it for many years. It's a great dish to pass at picnics and potlucks.

- 1/2 pound ground beef
- 1/2 pound ground pork
- 2 cans (14-1/2 ounces *each*) diced tomatoes
- 2 cups (8 ounces) shredded cheddar cheese
- 2 cups uncooked elbow macaroni
- 1 medium onion, finely chopped
- 1 cup frozen peas, thawed
- 2 cans (2-1/2 ounces *each*) sliced ripe olives, drained
- 1 jar (2 ounces) diced pimientos, drained
- 1 teaspoon salt
- 1/2 teaspoon paprika
- 1/4 teaspoon celery salt

In a large skillet, cook beef and pork over medium heat until no longer pink; drain. Add the remaining ingredients.

Transfer mixture to a greased 3-qt. baking dish. Bake, uncovered, at 350° for 1-1/2 hours or until the macaroni is tender, stirring every 30 minutes. **Yield:** 8 servings.

Editor's Note: If you're unable to find fresh ground pork for Two-Meat Macaroni, use 1/2 pound bulk pork sausage.

Baked Rice with Sausage

Baked Rice With Sausage

Naomi Flood, Emporia, Kansas

This recipe is perfect for potlucks or church suppers since it produces a big batch and has flavors with broad appeal. Most folks can't guess that the secret ingredient is chicken noodle soup mix.

- 2 pounds bulk Italian sausage
- 4 celery ribs, thinly sliced
- 1 large onion, chopped
- 1 large green pepper, chopped
- 4-1/2 cups water
- 3/4 cup dry chicken noodle soup mix
- 1 can (10-3/4 ounces) condensed cream of chicken soup, undiluted
- 1 cup uncooked long grain rice
- 1/4 cup dry bread crumbs
- 2 tablespoons butter, melted

In a large skillet, cook the sausage, celery, onion and green pepper over medium heat until meat is no longer pink and vegetables are tender; drain. In a large saucepan, bring water to a boil; add dry soup mix. Reduce heat; simmer, uncovered, for 5 minutes or until the noodles are tender. Stir in canned soup, rice and sausage mixture; mix well.

Transfer to a greased 13-in. x 9-in. x 2-in. baking dish. Cover and bake at 350° for 40 minutes. Toss bread crumbs and butter; sprinkle over rice mixture. Bake, uncovered, for 10-15 minutes or until rice is tender. Let stand for 10 minutes before serving. **Yield:** 12-14 servings.

Biscuit-Topped Beef N Beans

Triple-Onion Baked Potatoes (p. 48)

Chapter 3

Spuds on the Side

Like peas and carrots, meat and potatoes go hand in hand. That's why this chapter is stuffed with 51 side dishes for au gratin, twice-baked, mashed and other spud specialties.

Jalapeno Salsa Potatoes

Kim Lintner, Milwaukee, Wisconsin

This lively potato dish really adds a kick. It's another tasty way for my family to eat salsa—which we all enjoy—with or without tortilla chips. If you like recipes with some zip, you're sure to love it just as much as we do.

> 4 **large potatoes, peeled and cut widthwise into thirds**
> 1 **cup salsa**
> 1/3 **cup chopped onion**
> 12 **slices process American cheese**
> 1 **large jalapeno pepper, cut into 12 rings and seeded**

Place potatoes in a saucepan and cover with water; cover and bring to a boil. Cook until the potatoes are tender, about 20-30 minutes.

Drain and place potatoes in a greased 11-in. x 7-in. x 2-in. baking dish. Top with salsa, onion, cheese and jalapeno. Bake, uncovered, at 350° for 15-20 minutes or until the cheese is melted. **Yield:** 6 servings.

Editor's Note: When cutting or seeding hot peppers, use rubber or plastic gloves to protect your hands. Avoid touching your face.

Bacon Potato Bundles

Dorothy Sutherland, Seven Points, Texas

Cut cleanup by grilling these versatile potato bundles in foil packets. Wrap the bacon around the veggies and secure it with a toothpick for a fun presentation. Add carrots, squash or whatever vegetables you have on hand.

> 4 **large baking potatoes, peeled and quartered**
> 8 **onion slices**
> 8 **green pepper slices**
> 4 **bacon strips**

Salt and pepper to taste

Place the potatoes on four pieces of greased heavy-duty aluminum foil. Place onion and green pepper slices between potato quarters; top with bacon. Sprinkle with salt and pepper. Wrap in foil.

Grill, covered, over medium-high heat for 40-50 minutes or until the potatoes are tender, turning once. **Yield:** 4 servings.

Zesty Lemon Potatoes

Zesty Lemon Potatoes

Susan Mackenzie, Edwards, California

I created this recipe to go with fish, but it's also excellent with chicken and pork. The potatoes are good at room temperature or piping hot.

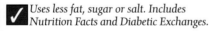
Uses less fat, sugar or salt. Includes Nutrition Facts and Diabetic Exchanges.

> 2 **medium red potatoes, cut into 1/2-inch cubes**
> 2 **teaspoons minced fresh parsley**
> 2 **teaspoons olive oil**
> 1 **teaspoon lemon juice**
> 1/2 **teaspoon grated lemon peel**
> 1/4 **teaspoon salt**
> 1/8 **teaspoon pepper**

Place potatoes in a saucepan and cover with water. Bring to a boil; cook until tender. In a bowl, combine the remaining ingredients. Drain potatoes; add the lemon mixture and toss to coat. **Yield:** 2 servings.

Nutrition Facts: 2/3 cup equals 114 calories, 5 g fat (1 g saturated fat), 0 cholesterol, 299 mg sodium, 15 g carbohydrate, 2 g fiber, 3 g protein. **Diabetic Exchanges:** 1 starch, 1/2 fat.

Pizza Potatoes

Kathy White, Chicopee, Massachusetts

For a simple side dish that's sure to appeal to kids, try this twist on traditional pizza. Packaged scalloped potatoes, canned tomatoes and pepperoni slices are combined for fast Italian fare that's delightfully different.

> 1 **package (5 ounces) scalloped potatoes**
> 1 **can (14-1/2 ounces) Italian stewed tomatoes**
> 1-1/2 **cups water**
> 1/4 **teaspoon dried oregano**
> 1 **package (3-1/2 ounces) sliced pepperoni**
> 1 **cup (4 ounces) shredded part-skim mozzarella cheese**

Combine the potatoes and contents of sauce mix in a greased 1-1/2-qt. baking dish. In a saucepan, bring tomatoes, water and oregano to a boil. Pour over potatoes. Top with pepperoni.

Bake, uncovered, at 375° for 50-60 minutes or until the potatoes are tender. Sprinkle with cheese. Bake 5-10 minutes longer or until cheese is melted. **Yield:** 4 servings.

Grilled Potato Skins

Mitzi Sentiff, Alexandria, Virginia

Everyone just raves about these delicious potato skins. They're nice to serve outside when you invite friends over for a grilled meal.

- 2 large baking potatoes
- 2 tablespoons butter, melted
- 2 teaspoons minced fresh rosemary *or* 1/2 teaspoon dried rosemary, crushed
- 1/2 teaspoon salt
- 1/2 teaspoon pepper
- 1 cup (4 ounces) shredded cheddar cheese
- 3 bacon strips, cooked and crumbled
- 2 green onions, chopped

Sour cream

Grilled Potato Skins

Cut each potato lengthwise into four wedges. Cut away the white portion, leaving 1/4 in. on the potato skins. Place skins on a microwave-safe plate. Microwave, uncovered, on high for 8-10 minutes or until tender. Combine the butter, rosemary, salt and pepper; brush over both sides of potato skins.

Grill potatoes, skin side up, uncovered, over direct medium heat for 2-3 minutes or until lightly browned. Turn potatoes and position over indirect heat; grill 2 minutes longer. Top with cheese. Cover and grill 2-3 minutes longer or until cheese is melted. Sprinkle with bacon and onions. Serve with sour cream. **Yield:** 8 appetizers.

Editor's Note: This recipe was tested in a 1,100-watt microwave.

Potato Chip Potatoes

Debra Hartze, Zeeland, North Dakota

Potato-lovers will thoroughly enjoy these can't-beat spuds that combine cubed potatoes and potato chips. My family requests it often, and I'm sure yours will, too!

- 6 medium potatoes, peeled and cut into 1/2-inch cubes
- 3/4 cup crushed potato chips, *divided*
- 1/2 cup chopped onion
- 2 tablespoons butter, melted
- 3/4 teaspoon salt
- 1/4 teaspoon pepper

In a large bowl, combine the potatoes, 1/2 cup of potato chips, onion, butter, salt and pepper; toss to combine.

Transfer to a greased shallow 2-qt. baking dish. Sprinkle with remaining potato chips. Bake, uncovered, at 350° for 40-50 minutes or until potatoes are tender. **Yield:** 6-8 servings.

Potato Chip Potatoes

Quick Tip

Add extra flavor to potato dishes with this simple seasoning blend. Fill a pint-size canning jar with a mixture of 1 cup salt, 1/4 cup pepper, 1/4 cup garlic powder and 1/8 cup onion powder.

Crumb-Coated Potato Halves

Crumb-Coated Potato Halves

Shirley Leister, West Chester, Pennsylvania

Dressing up potatoes is a snap with this easy method. What I like best about the recipe is that the potatoes are quick to assemble and I can pop them into the oven at the same time as my meat loaf.

1/2   cup seasoned bread crumbs
1   teaspoon paprika
1   teaspoon salt
1/8   teaspoon pepper
4   large potatoes, peeled and halved
2   tablespoons butter, melted

In a shallow bowl, combine the bread crumbs, paprika, salt and pepper. Brush potatoes with butter; roll in crumb mixture until coated.

Place potatoes in a greased 13-in. x 9-in. x 2-in. baking pan. Cover and bake at 350° for 1 hour or until the potatoes are tender. **Yield:** 6 servings.

Seasoned Oven Fries

Pat Fredericks, Oak Creek, Wisconsin

For a swift side these potato wedges are as tasty as the deep-fried versions but with less mess and fat. Watch your hungry bunch gobble them up.

6   medium baking potatoes
2   tablespoons butter, melted
2   tablespoons vegetable oil
1   teaspoon seasoned salt

Cut each potato lengthwise into thirds; cut each portion into thirds. In a large resealable plastic bag, combine the butter, oil and seasoned salt. Add potatoes; shake to coat.

Place the potatoes in a single layer on a greased baking sheet. Bake, uncovered, at 450° for 20-25 minutes or until the potatoes are tender, turning once. **Yield:** 6 servings.

Roasted Spicy Mustard Potatoes

Shirley A. Glaab, Hattiesburg, Mississippi

Even mild red potatoes can be a 'standout' side dish when they're tossed with this mustard and spice coating, then baked. Their delicious blend of seasonings perks up any meal.

✔ *Uses less fat, sugar or salt. Includes Nutrition Facts and Diabetic Exchanges.*

1/4   cup Dijon mustard
2   teaspoons paprika
1   teaspoon ground cumin
1   teaspoon chili powder
1/2   teaspoon salt
1/8   teaspoon cayenne pepper
2   pounds small red potatoes

Spray a shallow roasting pan with non-stick cooking spray three times to coat well; set aside.

In a large bowl, whisk the mustard, paprika, cumin, chili powder, salt and cayenne. Pierce potatoes with a fork several times; add to mustard mixture and toss to coat.

Place the covered potatoes in the prepared pan. Bake, uncovered, at 375° for 30-40 minutes or until the potatoes are tender. **Yield:** 8 servings.

Nutrition Facts: 1 serving equals 138 calories, 1 g fat (trace saturated fat), 0 cholesterol, 353 mg sodium, 30 g carbohydrate, 3 g fiber, 3 g protein. **Diabetic Exchange:** 2 starch.

Home-Style Scalloped Potatoes

Christine Eilerts, Tulsa, Oklahoma

The secret to a good scalloped potato dish is to make sure it has plenty of creamy sauce, which this recipe has. My husband and sons rate this can't-beat potato casserole the "best ever" and request it often.

1/3   cup chopped onion
5   tablespoons butter
5   tablespoons all-purpose flour
1-1/4   teaspoons salt
1/2   teaspoon pepper
5   cups milk
6   cups thinly sliced potatoes

In a large saucepan, saute onion in butter until tender. Stir in flour, salt and pepper until blended. Gradually add milk. Bring to a boil; cook and stir for 2 minutes or until sauce is thickened.

Place half of potatoes in a greased 3-qt. baking dish. Pour half of sauce over potatoes. Repeat layers. Bake, uncovered, at 350° for 60-70 minutes or until potatoes are tender and top is lightly browned. Serve immediately. **Yield:** 8 servings.

Quick Tip

Perk up scalloped potatoes by sprinkling a can of chopped green chilies between the layers of potatoes and sauce.

Potato Dumplings

Cathy Eland, Hightstown, New Jersey

With a few additional basic ingredients, my mom transformed potatoes into these delightful dumplings. This authentic German recipe is so hearty and comforting. We love the dumplings covered in sauerbraten gravy.

- **3 pounds russet potatoes**
- **2 eggs**
- **1 cup all-purpose flour,** *divided*
- **1/2 cup dry bread crumbs**
- **1 teaspoon salt**
- **1/4 teaspoon ground nutmeg**

Dash pepper

Minced fresh parsley, optional

Place potatoes in a saucepan and cover with water; bring to a boil. Reduce heat; cover and simmer for 30-35 minutes or until tender. Drain well. Refrigerate for 2 hours or overnight.

Peel and grate potatoes. In a bowl, combine the eggs, 3/4 cup flour, bread crumbs, salt, nutmeg and pepper. Add potatoes; mix with hands until well blended. Shape into 1-1/2-in. balls; roll in remaining flour.

In a large kettle, bring salted water to a boil. Add the dumplings, a few at a time, to boiling water. Simmer, uncovered, until the dumplings rise to the top; cook 2 minutes longer.

Remove dumplings with a slotted spoon to a serving bowl. Sprinkle with parsley if desired. **Yield:** 10 servings.

Roasted Garlic Mashed Potatoes

Rita Wenrich, La Luz, New Mexico

My family loves potatoes and considers this dressed-up version a real favorite. It makes the perfect sidekick to nearly any meal. The dish's mouth-watering flavor and memorable flair come from the tasty blend of roasted garlic and fresh rosemary.

- **2 whole garlic bulbs**
- **1 tablespoon olive oil**
- **6 medium baking potatoes, peeled and cubed**
- **1 cup milk plus 2 tablespoons milk**
- **2 tablespoons butter**
- **1 tablespoon minced fresh rosemary**
- **1 teaspoon salt**

Cut the top off garlic bulbs so each clove is exposed. Brush with oil; wrap in foil. Bake at 350° for 45 minutes or until garlic is very soft. Cool for 5 minutes. Remove garlic from skins; mash and set aside.

Place potatoes in a saucepan and cover with water. Bring to a boil; cover and cook for 20-25 minutes or until the potatoes very tender. Drain well.

Add milk, butter, rosemary, salt and garlic; mash until light and fluffy. **Yield:** 6 servings.

Roasted Garlic Mashed Potatoes

Old-Fashioned Potato Salad

Kathy Anderson, Wallkill, New York

This traditional potato salad recipe has been passed down through several generations in my mother's family. It's a satisfying addition to any family picnic or holiday meal.

- **5 pounds red potatoes**
- **1 cup sugar**
- **1 tablespoon all-purpose flour**
- **1 teaspoon salt**
- **1/2 teaspoon ground mustard**
- **1/4 teaspoon pepper**
- **3/4 cup white vinegar**
- **1/4 cup water**
- **3 eggs, lightly beaten**
- **1 cup thinly sliced green onions**
- **1-1/2 cups (12 ounces) sour cream**

Cook potatoes in boiling water until tender; drain and cool.

Meanwhile, in a saucepan, combine sugar, flour, salt, mustard and pepper. Add vinegar and water; bring to a boil. Boil and stir for 2 minutes. Add a small amount to eggs; return all to the pan.

Cook and stir for 1-1/2 to 2 minutes or until mixture is thickened and a thermometer reads 160°. Refrigerate until cooled.

Peel potatoes if desired; slice and place in a large bowl. Add onions. Stir sour cream into dressing; pour over potato mixture and toss to coat. **Yield:** 16-18 servings.

Potato Dumplings

West Coast Potato Salad

In a small bowl, combine the sour cream, mustard, thyme, tarragon and remaining lemon juice; fold into salad. Chill until serving. **Yield:** 12 servings.

Nutrition Facts: 1/2 cup (prepared with fat-free sour cream and without salt) equals 80 calories, 3 g fat (0 saturated fat), 1 mg cholesterol, 83 mg sodium, 11 g carbohydrate, 0 fiber, 3 g protein. **Diabetic Exchanges:** 1 vegetable, 1/2 starch, 1/2 fat.

Sweet Potato Wedges

Donna Howard, Stoughton, Wisconsin

Quartered sweet potatoes bake to perfection in a mildly spiced butter sauce. Leftovers reheat wonderfully to be enjoyed the second day.

- 3 **pounds sweet potatoes, peeled and quartered lengthwise (about 10 cups)**
- 6 **tablespoons butter, melted**
- 6 **tablespoons orange juice**
- 3/4 **teaspoon salt**
- 3/4 **teaspoon ground cinnamon**

Arrange sweet potatoes in a greased 13-in. x 9-in. x 2-in. baking dish. Combine the butter, orange juice, salt and cinnamon; drizzle over sweet potatoes. Cover and bake at 350° for 55-60 minutes or until potatoes are tender. **Yield:** 10 servings (8 cups).

Broccoli Potato Supreme

Jane Birch, Edison, New Jersey

My family insists that this two-in-one dish makes an appearance at all of our special meals. Every bite is doubly delicious!

- 3 **cups hot mashed potatoes**
- 1 **package (3 ounces) cream cheese, softened**
- 1/4 **cup milk**
- 1 **egg**
- 2 **tablespoons butter, softened**
- 1/2 **teaspoon salt**
- 1/4 **teaspoon pepper**
- 1 **can (2.8 ounces) french-fried onions,** *divided*
- 4-1/2 **cups fresh broccoli florets**
- 1 **cup (4 ounces) shredded cheddar cheese**

In a mixing bowl, combine the first seven ingredients; beat until smooth. Fold in half of the onions. Spread onto the bottom and up the sides of a greased 13-in. x 9-in. x 2-in. baking dish, forming a shell. Bake, uncovered, at 350° for 20-25 minutes or until edges are lightly browned.

Cook broccoli in a small amount of water until crisp-tender; drain. Place in the potato shell. Sprinkle with cheese and remaining onions. Bake 10 minutes longer. **Yield:** 8 servings.

West Coast Potato Salad

West Coast Potato Salad

Phyllis Lee Ciardo, Albany, California

This potato salad incorporates tender asparagus and the tongue-tingling tang of herbs and lemon juice. Here in the San Francisco Bay area, which is close to the state's primary asparagus-growing region, we look forward to spring and this fresh vegetable.

✓ *Uses less fat, sugar or salt. Includes Nutrition Facts and Diabetic Exchanges.*

- 1-1/2 **pounds medium red potatoes, cooked and peeled**
- 1/4 **cup chopped green onions**
- 4 **tablespoons lemon juice,** *divided*
- 2 **tablespoons vegetable oil**
- 2 **tablespoons minced fresh parsley**
- 1/2 **teaspoon salt, optional**
- 1/4 **teaspoon pepper**
- 3/4 **cup thinly sliced celery**
- 1 **pound fresh asparagus, cut into 3/4-inch pieces**
- 1/2 **cup sour cream**
- 2 **tablespoons Dijon mustard**
- 1 **teaspoon dried thyme**
- 1 **teaspoon dried tarragon**

Place potatoes in a large bowl and set aside. In a jar with tight-fitting lid, combine onions, 3 tablespoons lemon juice, oil, parsley, salt if desired and pepper; shake well. Pour over potatoes and toss gently. Add celery; set aside.

In a large saucepan, bring 1/2 in. of water to a boil. Add asparagus; cover and boil for 3 minutes. Drain and immediately place asparagus in ice water. Drain and pat dry. Add to potato mixture.

Broccoli Potato Supreme

Twice-as-Nice Mashed Potatoes

Kerry Schroeppel, Springfield, Missouri

If you can't decide what kind of potatoes to serve, reach for this recipe, which blends both red and sweet potatoes. It will quickly become a staple at your family dinners.

✓ *Uses less fat, sugar or salt. Includes Nutrition Facts.*

- 1 large whole garlic bulb
- 2 tablespoons olive oil
- 1-1/2 pounds red potatoes, peeled and cubed
- 1-1/2 pounds sweet potatoes, peeled and cubed
- 1/2 cup milk
- 1/4 cup butter, softened
- 1/2 teaspoon dried rosemary, crushed
- 1/3 cup grated Parmesan cheese

Salt and pepper to taste

Remove papery outer skin from garlic (do not peel or separate cloves). Brush with oil. Wrap bulb in heavy-duty foil. Bake at 425° for 30-35 minutes or until softened. Cool for 10-15 minutes; peel garlic and reserve oil. Reduce heat to 400°.

Place red and sweet potatoes in separate saucepans; cover with water. Bring to a boil. Reduce heat; cover and cook for 15-20 minutes or until very tender. Drain.

Place both potatoes in a large mixing bowl. Add the milk, butter, rosemary, roasted garlic and reserved oil. Stir in Parmesan cheese, salt and pepper.

Transfer to a greased 1-1/2-qt. baking dish. Cover and bake for 25-30 minutes or until heated through. **Yield:** 6-8 servings.

Nutrition Facts: 3/4 cup equals 242 calories, 11 g fat (5 g saturated fat), 20 mg cholesterol, 170 mg sodium, 32 g carbohydrate, 4 g fiber, 4 g protein.

Twice-as-Nice Mashed Potatoes

Grilled Onion Potatoes

Janet Gioia, Broadalbin, New York

My mother often fixed these potatoes when we grilled outdoors during the warm summer months. The tasty treatment requires just a few ingredients, so you can have them sizzling on the grill in no time at all.

- 5 medium baking potatoes
- 1 small onion, sliced

Salt and pepper to taste

1 bottle (8 ounces) zesty Italian salad dressing

Cut each potato into five slices. Place onion between slices and sprinkle with salt and pepper. Reassemble each potato; place on a double layer of heavy-duty foil (about 12 in. square).

Pour 2-4 tablespoons of salad dressing over each potato. Wrap foil around potatoes and seal tightly. Grill, covered, over medium heat for 50-60 minutes or until the potatoes are tender. **Yield:** 5 servings.

Teriyaki Potatoes

Sue Jent, Golcolda, Illinois

Simple seasonings turn red potatoes into a special side that's attractive, too. They are so easy to prepare that you can have them on the table in about 15 minutes.

✓ *Uses less fat, sugar or salt. Includes Nutrition Facts and Diabetic Exchanges.*

- 1-1/2 pounds small red potatoes, quartered
- 1 tablespoon butter
- 1 tablespoon teriyaki *or* soy sauce
- 1/4 teaspoon garlic salt, optional
- 1/4 teaspoon Italian seasoning

Dash *each* pepper and cayenne pepper

Place the potatoes in an ungreased 1-1/2-qt. microwave-safe dish. Dot with butter. Add remaining ingredients; toss to coat. Cover and microwave on high for 7-10 minutes or until potatoes are tender, stirring twice. **Yield:** 6 servings.

Nutrition Facts: 1 serving (prepared without garlic salt) equals 93 calories, 2 g fat (0 saturated fat), 0 cholesterol, 26 mg sodium, 15 g carbohydrate, 0 fiber, 3 g protein. **Diabetic Exchanges:** 1 starch, 1/2 fat.

Editor's Note: This recipe was tested in a 1,100-watt microwave.

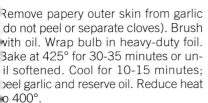

Quick Tip

Instead of adding milk to mashed potatoes, reserve some of the water used to boil the potatoes and mix in powdered milk. This retains the nutrients and potato-flavor in the water.

Slow Cooker Mashed Potatoes

Double Cheddar Hash Browns

Renee Hatfield, Marshallville, Ohio

This comforting side dish starts with convenient frozen hash browns and canned soups. Shredded cheddar cheese and crunchy cornflake crumbs are the fast finishing touch to this yummy potato bake.

  1 **can (10-3/4 ounces) condensed cream of onion soup, undiluted**
  1 **can (10-3/4 ounces) condensed cheddar cheese soup, undiluted**
  1 **package (30 ounces) frozen shredded hash brown potatoes**
  2 **cups (8 ounces) shredded cheddar cheese**
  1 **cup crushed cornflakes**

In a large bowl, combine the soups. Stir in hash browns. Pour into a greased 2-1/2-qt. baking dish. Sprinkle with cheese and cornflake crumbs.

    Cover and bake potatoes at 350° for 50 minutes. Uncover; bake 10 minutes longer or until the top is golden. **Yield:** 8 servings.

Cheddar Mushroom Potatoes

Jacqueline Graves, Lawrenceville, Georgia

When they were little, our children loved this cheesy dish. After an adult has sliced the potatoes, youngsters can do the rest. Overlapping the potatoes in the baking dish to create a pretty pattern is half the fun.

  4 **medium potatoes, cut into 1/4-inch slices**
  1 **cup (4 ounces) shredded cheddar cheese**
  1 **can (10-3/4 ounces) condensed cream of mushroom soup, undiluted**
1/2 **teaspoon paprika**
1/4 **teaspoon pepper**

Arrange potatoes in a greased shallow 2-qt. baking dish; sprinkle with cheese. In a bowl, combine soup, paprika and pepper; spread over cheese.

    Cover and bake at 400° for 45 minutes. Uncover; bake 10 minutes longer or until the potatoes are tender. **Yield:** 4-6 servings.

Slow Cooker Mashed Potatoes

Trudy Vincent, Valles Mines, Missouri

Sour cream and cream cheese add richness to these smooth, make-ahead potatoes. They're wonderful when time is tight because they don't require any last-minute mashing.

  1 **package (3 ounces) cream cheese, softened**
1/2 **cup sour cream**
1/4 **cup butter, softened**
  1 **envelope ranch salad dressing mix**
  1 **teaspoon dried parsley flakes**
  6 **cups warm mashed potatoes (without added milk and butter)**

In a large bowl, combine the cream cheese, sour cream, butter, salad dressing mix and parsley; stir in mashed potatoes. Transfer to a 3-qt. slow cooker. Cover and cook on low for 2-4 hours. **Yield:** 8-10 servings.

    Editor's Note: This recipe was tested with fresh potatoes (not instant) in a slow cooker with heating elements surrounding the unit, not only in the base.

Double Cheddar Hash Browns

Fiesta Potatoes

Socorro Kimble, Bakersfield, California

I originally served this zippy filling on open-faced French rolls. One day I added some of the leftover mixture to my baked potato at dinner. What a treat! Now I make these flavorful potatoes often.

- 4 medium potatoes, baked
- 1/2 cup sour cream
- 1/2 cup diced fully cooked ham
- 3 tablespoons grated Parmesan cheese
- 2 tablespoons mayonnaise
- 1 to 2 tablespoons chopped green chilies

Salt and pepper to taste
- 1 cup (4 ounces) shredded sharp cheddar cheese

Place potatoes in a 13-in. x 9-in. x 2-in. baking dish. With a sharp knife, cut an X in the top of each potato. Bake, uncovered, at 350° for 10 minutes or until warm.

Meanwhile, combine the sour cream, ham, Parmesan cheese, mayonnaise, chilies, salt and pepper; mix well. Fluff potato pulp with a fork. Top with ham mixture; sprinkle with cheese.

Bake, uncovered, 10-15 minutes longer or until cheese is melted. **Yield:** 4 servings.

Editor's Note: If using hot baked potatoes, omit the baking time before adding the topping.

Garlic Potato Balls

Quick Tip

Generally, three medium russet potatoes or eight to ten small new potatoes equal 1 pound. If you usually purchase the same types of potatoes, weigh them in the produce section of your store so you know what one pound of your favorite variety is.

Cheesy Cottage Potatoes

**Mary Louise Ireland
New Wilmington, Pennsylvania**

This home-style recipe is a real winner. Not only does my family like it, but it's popular at potlucks. It's also great to serve at a dinner with friends. Just remove it from the refrigerator 30 minutes before baking.

- 3 slices bread, crusts removed and cubed
- 1/2 cup milk
- 10 medium potatoes, peeled, cubed and cooked
- 2 medium green peppers, chopped
- 1 large onion, chopped
- 1/2 cup minced fresh parsley
- 1-1/2 pounds process cheese (Velveeta), cubed
- 1/4 cup butter, melted

In a small bowl, soak bread in milk; set aside. In a large bowl, combine the potatoes, green peppers, onion, parsley and the reserved bread mixture. Stir in the cheese.

Transfer mixture to a greased 13-in. x 9-in. x 2-in. baking dish. Drizzle with butter. Bake, uncovered, at 350° for 35-40 minutes or until bubbly. **Yield:** 16-20 servings.

Garlic Potato Balls

Alpha Wilson, Roswell, New Mexico

I've used this recipe since I was married. Both my husband and I worked, and we liked to have hearty meat-and-potato meals when we came home in the evening. This side was easy and quick to make on busy days. Sized right for two, there were never any leftovers.

- 1 tablespoon butter
- 1 can (15 ounces) small white potatoes, drained
- 1/4 teaspoon garlic salt
- 1/2 teaspoon minced fresh parsley

In a skillet, melt butter over medium heat. Add potatoes; sprinkle with garlic salt. Cook and stir for 15-18 minutes or until golden brown. Sprinkle with parsley. **Yield:** 2 servings.

Grilled Sweet Potatoes

Gay Nell Nicholas, Henderson, Texas

My husband and I love these sweet spuds any way they are cooked. This recipe is not only different, it's delicious, too. Sweet potato wedges are seasoned to please in this savory side dish.

 Uses less fat, sugar or salt. Includes Nutrition Facts and Diabetic Exchanges.

- 2 **pounds sweet potatoes, peeled and cut into wedges**
- 3 **tablespoons reduced-sodium soy sauce**
- 2 **tablespoons sherry *or* apple juice**
- 2 **tablespoons honey**
- 2 **tablespoons water**
- 1 **garlic clove, minced**
- 1 **tablespoon sesame oil**

Place the sweet potatoes in a steamer basket; place in a saucepan over 1 in. of water. Bring to a boil; cover and steam for 5-7 minutes.

Place potatoes in a large bowl. In another bowl, combine the soy sauce, sherry or juice, honey, water and garlic; pour over potatoes and toss gently.

Drain sweet potatoes, reserving soy sauce mixture. Arrange sweet potatoes in a single layer in a grill basket coated with nonstick cooking spray. Brush potatoes with oil. Grill, covered, over medium heat for 8-10 minutes or until tender, basting with reserved soy sauce mixture and turning occasionally. **Yield:** 8 servings.

Nutrition Facts: 1 serving equals 158 calories, 2 g fat (trace saturated fat), 0 cholesterol, 242 mg sodium, 33 g carbohydrate, 2 g fiber, 2 g protein. **Diabetic Exchange:** 2 starch.

Triple-Onion Baked Potatoes

Triple-Onion Baked Potatoes

Char Shanahan, Schererville, Indiana

I've been making twice-baked potatoes for many years, and I'm constantly changing my recipe. This version features a rich filling of onions, bacon, sour cream and cheese. I like to serve these potatoes with baked ham.

- 4 **large baking potatoes**
- 1 **pound sliced bacon, diced**
- 1/2 **cup finely chopped red onion**
- 1/2 **cup finely chopped yellow onion**
- 1/2 **cup sour cream**
- 2 **tablespoons milk**
- 1 **cup diced American cheese**
- 1/2 **cup shredded cheddar cheese**
- 4 **green onions, finely sliced**

Bake potatoes at 400° for 1 hour or until tender.

Meanwhile, in a large skillet, cook the bacon over medium heat until crisp; remove to paper towels. Drain, reserving 1 tablespoon drippings. In the drippings, saute red and yellow onions until tender; set aside.

When potatoes are cool enough to handle, cut in half lengthwise. Scoop out pulp, leaving an 1/8-in. shell. In a mixing bowl, beat the pulp, sour cream and milk until creamy. Stir in sauteed onions, American cheese and 1 cup of bacon. Spoon into potato shells.

Place on a baking sheet. Bake at 400° for 25 minutes. Sprinkle with cheddar cheese, green onions and remaining bacon. Bake potatoes 5-10 minutes longer or until cheese is melted. **Yield:** 8 servings.

Quick Tip

Help your potatoes last longer. To keep potatoes from sprouting before you use them, place an apple in the bag with the potatoes.

Jalapeno Potato Salad

Sarah Woodruff, Watertown, South Dakota

Try putting this zippy spin on potato salad. Jalapeno peppers, spicy brown mustard and a blend of seasonings give it an irresistible kick. It's perfect for a picnic or backyard barbecue!

- 6 medium red potatoes, peeled and cubed
- 2 celery ribs, chopped
- 2 hard-cooked eggs, chopped
- 1/4 cup chopped onion
- 2 small jalapeno peppers, seeded and chopped
- 1/4 cup mayonnaise
- 3 tablespoons spicy brown mustard
- 3 teaspoons hot pepper sauce
- 1/4 teaspoon ground cumin
- 1/4 teaspoon pepper

Place the potatoes in a large saucepan and cover with water. Bring to a boil. Reduce heat; cover and cook for 10-15 minutes or until tender. Drain; cool to room temperature.

In a large serving bowl, combine potatoes, celery, eggs, onion and jalapenos. In a small bowl, combine the mayonnaise, mustard, hot pepper sauce, cumin and pepper.

Pour over potato mixture and toss gently to coat. Cover and refrigerate overnight. **Yield:** 5 servings.

Editor's Note: When cutting or seeding hot peppers, use rubber or plastic gloves to protect your hands. Avoid touching your face.

Cubed Parmesan Potatoes

Jalapeno Potato Salad

Cubed Parmesan Potatoes

Sarah Reinsch, Geneva, Nebraska

I created this potato dish myself. I often cook according to what I have on hand, so the ingredients are staples. This recipe is easy to prepare and compatible with a variety of entrees.

- 2 tablespoons butter, melted
- 1 teaspoon lemon juice
- 2 medium baking potatoes, peeled and cubed
- 1/4 cup grated Parmesan cheese
- 1/2 teaspoon seasoned salt
- 1/4 teaspoon pepper

Dried parsley flakes

In a 1-qt. microwave-safe dish, combine butter and lemon juice. Add potatoes; toss to coat. Sprinkle with Parmesan cheese, seasoned salt and pepper; toss to coat. Cover dish and microwave on high for 3-5 minutes or until the potatoes are tender, turning once. Let stand for 5 minutes. Sprinkle with parsley. **Yield:** 2 servings.

Editor's Note: This recipe was tested in a 1,100-watt microwave. To bake instead, place the potato mixture in a greased 8-in. square baking dish. Bake, uncovered, at 400° for 20-25 minutes or until tender.

Cheddar Taters

Cheddar Taters

Ruth Van Nattan, Kingston, Tennessee

Potato chips are the fun topping sprinkled over this irresistible treatment for Tater Tots. With its garlic, onion and cheese flavors, you're not likely to have much left over. To cut preparation and cleanup time, try mixing the ingredients right in the baking dish.

> 1 **can (10-3/4 ounces) condensed cream of chicken soup, undiluted**
> 1 **can (12 ounces) evaporated milk**
> 1 **cup (8 ounces) sour cream**
> 1/2 **cup butter, melted**
> 1 **teaspoon garlic powder**
> 1 **teaspoon onion powder**
> 1 **package (32 ounces) frozen Tater Tots**
> 1-1/2 **cups (6 ounces) shredded cheddar cheese**
> 1 **cup crushed potato chips**

In a large bowl, combine the first six ingredients. Gently stir in the Tater Tots. Transfer to a greased 13-in. x 9-in. x 2-in. baking dish. Sprinkle with cheese and potato chips. Bake, uncovered, at 350° for 30-35 minutes or until bubbly. **Yield:** 8-10 servings.

Seasoned French Fries

Sharon Crider, Stoughton, Wisconsin

These simple, fuss-free spuds come together easily with frozen crinkle-cut fries and just a few other ingredients. They're perfect paired with a hamburger, sandwich or hot dog.

> 5 **cups frozen crinkle-cut french fries**
> 1 **teaspoon onion salt**
> 1/4 **teaspoon paprika**
> 1/3 **cup grated Parmesan cheese**

Arrange the french fries in a greased 15-in. x 10-in. x 1-in. baking pan. Sprinkle with onion salt and paprika; toss to coat. Bake fries at 450° for 15-20 minutes or until lightly browned. Sprinkle fries with Parmesan cheese; toss to coat. **Yield:** 4 servings.

Twice-Baked Spuds

Dominic Spano, Colonie, New York

These satisfying potatoes are nutritious and can be prepared a day ahead to save you time. Simply keep spuds refrigerated and bake before serving.

> 2 **large baking potatoes**
> 1 **cup chopped peeled parsnips**
> 1 **garlic clove, peeled**
> 2 **tablespoons cream cheese, softened**
> 2 **tablespoons buttermilk**
> 1/2 **teaspoon salt**

Pinch pepper

Dash hot pepper sauce

> 1/4 **cup finely chopped green onions**
> 1 **tablespoon grated Parmesan cheese**
> 1/8 **teaspoon paprika**

Bake potatoes at 375° for 1 hour or until tender. Allow to cool. Place parsnips and garlic in a small saucepan; cover with water. Bring to a boil over medium heat. Reduce heat; cover and simmer for 20 minutes or until tender. Drain and mash.

Cut a thin slice off the top of each potato; discard top. Scoop out the pulp, leaving a thin shell. In a bowl, mash the potato pulp with parsnips and garlic. Beat in next five ingredients, using a hand mixer.

Stir in green onions. Spoon into the potato shells. Combine the Parmesan cheese and paprika; sprinkle over top. Place on a baking sheet. Bake, uncovered, at 375° for 20-30 minutes or until heated through. **Yield:** 2 servings.

Twice-Baked Spuds

Deep-Fried Potato Skins

Deep-Fried Potato Skins

Leslie Cunnian, Peterborough, Ontario

The combination of potatoes, cheese, bacon and garlic dip in this recipe is fantastic. The skins can be served as a side with roast prime rib or any other meat you choose. You can also try them as warm appetizer.

    4 **large baking potatoes**
    2 **cups (16 ounces) sour cream**
    1 **envelope onion soup mix**
    1 **tablespoon finely chopped onion**
    5 **garlic cloves, minced**
Dash hot pepper sauce
Oil for deep-fat frying
  1/2 **cup shredded cheddar cheese**
  1/2 **cup shredded Swiss cheese**
    6 **to 8 bacon strips, cooked and crumbled**
    4 **teaspoons minced chives *or* green onion**

Bake potatoes at 400° for 1 hour or until potatoes are tender.

Meanwhile, for dip, combine the sour cream, soup mix, onion, garlic and hot pepper sauce in a bowl. Cover and refrigerate until serving.

When potatoes are cool enough to handle, cut in half lengthwise. Scoop out pulp, leaving a 1/4-in. shell (dicard or save pulp for another use). With a scissors, cut each potato half into three lengthwise strips.

In an electric skillet or deep-fat fryer, heat oil to 375°. Fry skins in oil for 2-3 minutes or until golden brown and crisp.

Place the potato skins in a 15-in. x 10-in. x 1-in. baking pan. Combine the cheeses and bacon; sprinkle over potatoes. Broil 4 in. from the heat for 1-2 minutes or until cheese is melted. Sprinkle with chives. Serve with the dip. **Yield:** 2 dozen.

Bacon Cheese Fries

Marilyn Dutkus, Laguna Beach, California

These tempting potatoes are one finger food I can make a meal of. Quick to fix and hearty, they're a hit at parties or as a snack. Bottled ranch salad dressing is a tasty alternative to sour cream.

    1 **package (32 ounces) frozen French fried potatoes**
    1 **cup (4 ounces) shredded cheddar cheese**
  1/2 **cup thinly sliced green onions**
  1/4 **cup crumbled cooked bacon**
Ranch salad dressing

Cook French fries according to package directions. Place the fries on a broiler-proof dish or platter. Sprinkle with cheese, onions and bacon. Broil french fries for 1-2 minutes or until cheese is melted. Serve with ranch dressing. **Yield:** 8-10 servings.

Bacon Cheese Fries

Mashed Potatoes With Carrot

Larry Stine, Brookings, South Dakota

One day, I wanted to make my mashed potatoes more interesting, so I added a carrot and some onion. This delightful dish goes well with and adds color to any entree.

    2 **medium potatoes, peeled and quartered**
    1 **medium carrot, peeled and chopped**
  1/4 **cup chopped onion**
    2 **tablespoons heavy whipping cream**
    1 **tablespoon butter**
  1/4 **teaspoon salt**
  1/8 **teaspoon pepper**
Pinch sugar

Place the vegetables in a saucepan, cover with water. Bring to a boil. Reduce heat; cover and simmer for 12-15 minutes or until the vegetables are tender.

Drain and place vegetables in a mixing bowl; mash until smooth. Add the cream, butter, salt, pepper and sugar; mix well. **Yield:** 2 servings.

Camp Potatoes

JoAnn Dettbarn, Brainerd, Minnesota

The onion, cheddar cheese and Worcestershire sauce combine to make a super side dish for any grilled meat. Plus, cooking in the foil makes cleanup a breeze.

> 5 medium potatoes, peeled and thinly sliced
> 1 medium onion, sliced
> 6 tablespoons butter
> 1/3 cup shredded cheddar cheese
> 2 tablespoons minced fresh parsley
> 1 tablespoon Worcestershire sauce
> Salt and pepper to taste
> 1/3 cup chicken broth

Place the potatoes and onion on a large piece of heavy-duty foil (about 20 in. x 20 in.); dot with butter. Combine the cheese, parsley, Worcestershire sauce, salt and pepper; sprinkle over potatoes.

Fold foil up around potatoes and add broth. Seal the edges of foil well. Grill, covered, over medium heat for 35-40 minutes or until potatoes are tender. **Yield:** 4-6 servings.

Sweet Potato Apple Salad

Camp Potatoes

Sweet Potato Apple Salad

Dorothy Smith, El Dorado, Arkansas

Pairing a seasonal fruit and vegetable makes for a very pretty and unusual salad to accompany a turkey dinner. The poppy seed dressing has a citrus tang and really brings out the flavor. If you're looking for a different dish, give this one a try!

> 6 medium sweet potatoes (about 2-1/2 pounds)
> 1/2 cup olive oil
> 1/4 cup orange juice
> 1 tablespoon sugar
> 1 tablespoon white wine vinegar
> 1 tablespoon Dijon mustard
> 1 tablespoon finely chopped onion
> 1-1/2 teaspoons poppy seeds
> 1 teaspoon grated orange peel
> 1/2 teaspoon grated lemon peel
> 2 medium tart apples (about 3/4 pound), chopped
> 2 green onions, thinly sliced

In a large saucepan, cook sweet potatoes in boiling salted water until just tender, about 20 minutes. Cool the potatoes completely.

Meanwhile, in a jar with a tight-fitting lid, combine the next nine ingredients; shake well. Peel potatoes; cut each potato in half lengthwise, then into 1/2-in. slices.

In a 4-qt. bowl, layer a fourth of the sweet potatoes, apples and onions; drizzle with a fourth of the salad dressing. Repeat layers three times. Refrigerate for 1-2 hours. Toss before serving. **Yield:** 8-10 servings.

German Potato Casserole

Dara Luburgh, Sparta, New Jersey

I bring this side to an annual Oktoberfest party. Everyone likes it, which ensures our invitation back year after year. There are never any leftovers to bring home.

- 5 pounds red potatoes, peeled and cut into 1/2-inch cubes
- 1 pound sliced bacon, diced
- 8 hard-cooked eggs, chopped
- 1 large onion, chopped
- 1/2 teaspoon salt
- 1/2 teaspoon pepper
- 1-1/2 cups mayonnaise
- 3 tablespoons cider vinegar
- 2 tablespoons Worcestershire sauce
- 1 pound process cheese (Velveeta), cubed

Place potatoes in a Dutch oven and cover with water. Bring to a boil. Reduce heat; cover and cook for 15-20 minutes or until tender. Drain.

In a skillet, cook bacon over medium heat until crisp. Using a slotted spoon, remove to paper towels; drain, reserving 1 tablespoon drippings.

In a large bowl, gently toss the potatoes, bacon, eggs, onion, salt and pepper. Combine the mayonnaise, vinegar, Worcestershire sauce and reserved bacon drippings; add to potato mixture and toss to coat.

Divide half of the mixture between one greased 13-in. x 9-in. x 2-in. baking dish and one 9-in. square baking dish. Top with half of the cheese cubes. Repeat layers. Bake, uncovered, at 350° for 40-45 minutes or until golden brown and bubbly. **Yield:** 16-20 servings.

Editor's Note: Reduced-fat or fat-free mayonnaise is not recommended for this recipe.

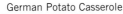
German Potato Casserole

Roasted Fan-Shaped Potatoes

Roasted Fan-Shaped Potatoes

Eunice Stoen, Decorah, Iowa

These wonderful oven-roasted potatoes are very pretty to serve—the partially cut slices spread out in the shape of a fan. They're fun to bring to a potluck as folks can easily take as many slices as they want.

- 12 large baking potatoes
- 1/2 teaspoon salt
- 1/2 cup butter, melted, *divided*
- 6 tablespoons dry bread crumbs
- 6 tablespoons shredded Parmesan cheese

With a sharp knife, slice potatoes thinly but not all the way through, leaving slices attached at the bottom. Place the potatoes in a greased shallow baking dish. Sprinkle potatoes with salt; brush with 1/4 cup butter. Bake, uncovered, at 425° for 30 minutes.

Brush potatoes with remaining butter and sprinkle with bread crumbs. Bake 20 minutes longer. Sprinkle with Parmesan cheese. Bake 5-10 minutes more or until potatoes are tender and golden brown. **Yield:** 12 servings.

Quick Tip

When boiling potatoes, drop a pea-size dab of butter or margarine into the water as it comes to a boil. This will prevent the foam that forms and would otherwise boil over the pot.

Western Cubed Potatoes

Karen Darrell, Bethalto, Illinois

Serve these zesty potatoes to give any potluck a kick. The tasty blend of seasonings and chopped green chilies will keep people coming back for more.

- **1/2** cup butter, melted
- **1** can (4 ounces) chopped green chilies
- **2** tablespoons finely chopped onion
- **1/2** teaspoon salt
- **1/4** teaspoon garlic salt
- **1/4** teaspoon pepper
- **6** medium potatoes, cubed
- **1/4** cup minced fresh parsley

In a large bowl, combine the first six ingredients. Add the potatoes and toss to coat. Transfer potatoes to an ungreased 2-qt. baking dish.

Cover and bake at 350° for 45 minutes. Uncover; bake 20-25 minutes longer or until the potatoes are tender. Sprinkle the potatoes with parsley. **Yield:** 6 servings.

Home-Style Mashed Potatoes

Christine Wilson, Sellersville, Pennsylvania

Leaving the tender skins on the spuds not only saves time, it sparks the flavor and adds pretty color to these hearty mashed potatoes. They are perfect with a pork roast and versatile enough to go well with other entrees, like chicken or beef.

- **3** pounds red potatoes, quartered
- **2** teaspoons salt, *divided*
- **1/4** to 1/2 cup milk
- **5** tablespoons butter
- **1/4** teaspoon white pepper

Place the potatoes in a large saucepan or Dutch oven; cover with water. Add 1 teaspoon salt. Cover and bring to a boil. Reduce heat; cook for 20-30 minutes or until very tender.

Drain potatoes well and place in a large mixing bowl. Add 1/4 cup milk, butter, pepper and remaining salt. Beat on low speed until potatoes are light and fluffy, adding remaining milk if needed. **Yield:** 8 servings.

Home-Style Mashed Potatoes

Creamy Hash Brown Bake

Yvonne Nave, Lyons, Kansas

This creamy casserole side couldn't be much easier to prepare. I just mix the ingredients together and sprinkle crushed potato chips on top. The end result is so satisfying that some people even enjoy the potato bake as a meatless entree.

- **1** can (10-3/4 ounces) condensed cream of mushroom soup, undiluted
- **1** can (10-3/4 ounces) condensed cheddar cheese soup, undiluted
- **1** cup (8 ounces) sour cream
- **1/2** cup butter, softened
- **1/4** cup chopped onion
- **1/2** teaspoon salt
- **1** package (28 ounces) frozen O'Brien hash brown potatoes
- **3/4** cup crushed potato chips

In a large bowl, combine the soups, sour cream, butter, onion and salt. Add potatoes; mix well.

Pour the potato mixture into a greased 13-in. x 9-in. x 2-in. baking dish. Sprinkle top with potato chips.

Bake, uncovered, at 350° for 55-60 minutes or until the potatoes are tender. **Yield:** 10-12 servings.

Western Cubed Potatoes

Alfredo Potatoes

Peter Barry, Norrisville, Maryland

These stuffed potatoes are a great way to round out a meal or serve as a meal alone. Cut the recipe in half and use a small potato for a winning after-school snack.

- 2 large baking potatoes
- 1 cup prepared Alfredo sauce
- 1 teaspoon garlic powder
- 1/2 teaspoon pepper
- 1/8 teaspoon dried thyme
- 1 cup (4 ounces) shredded cheddar cheese, *divided*
- 1/2 cup shredded part-skim mozzarella cheese

Pierce potatoes several times with a fork and place on a microwave-safe plate. Microwave on high for 4-1/2 minutes or until tender. Allow potatoes to cool slightly.

Meanwhile, in a bowl, combine the Alfredo sauce, garlic powder, pepper and thyme. Stir in 1/2 cup cheddar cheese and mozzarella cheese. Cut potatoes in half lengthwise. Scoop out the pulp and add to the sauce mixture; mix well. Spoon into potato shells.

Sprinkle with remaining cheddar cheese. Microwave on high for 45 seconds or until cheese is melted. **Yield:** 4 servings.

Editor's Note: This recipe was tested in a 1,100-watt microwave.

Alfredo Potatoes

Colby Hash Browns

Kimberly Lund, Park City, Kansas

If your gang likes bubbling hot casseroles, you're going to love this cheesy side dish. Try it alongside pork chops, chicken or even as an addition to breakfast or brunch.

- 1 cup milk
- 1/2 cup beef broth
- 2 tablespoons butter, melted, *divided*
- 1 teaspoon salt
- 1/4 teaspoon pepper

Dash garlic powder

- 1 package (30 ounces) frozen country-style shredded hash brown potatoes
- 2 cups (8 ounces) shredded Colby cheese

In a large bowl, combine the milk, broth, 1 tablespoon butter, salt, pepper and garlic powder. Stir in hash browns. Heat remaining butter in a large nonstick skillet. Add hash brown mixture. Cook and stir over medium heat until potatoes are heated through. Stir in cheese.

Transfer to a greased shallow 2-qt. baking dish. Bake, uncovered, at 350° for 40-45 minutes or until potatoes are tender. **Yield:** 6 servings.

Colby Hash Browns

Quick Tip

To speed dinner prep, zap potatoes in the microwave for 10 minutes before setting them on the grill with your entree. You'll enjoy the spuds' flame-broiled flavor with less wait.

Twice-Baked Ranch Potatoes

Janice Arnold, Gansevoort, New York

I make the most of leftover mashed potatoes to create these zippy stuffed potatoes. You can enjoy two and store the other two in the freezer. They warm up nicely in the microwave for later.

- 4 large baking potatoes (about 2-1/4 pounds)
- 1 package (3 ounces) cream cheese, softened
- 2 tablespoons milk
- 1 envelope (1 ounce) ranch salad dressing mix
- 1-1/2 cups mashed potatoes
- 1/4 cup shredded cheddar cheese

Scrub and pierce potatoes; place on a microwave-safe plate. Microwave, uncovered, on high for 13-15 minutes or until tender, turning several times. Let stand for 10 minutes.

Meanwhile, in a small mixing bowl, combine cream cheese and milk; beat in salad dressing mix. Add mashed potatoes; mix well. Cut a thin slice from the top of each potato; scoop out pulp, leaving a thin shell. Add pulp to the cream cheese mixture and mash. Spoon into potato shells. Top with cheese.

Place two potatoes on a microwave-safe plate. Microwave, uncovered, on high for 3-1/2 to 4-1/2 minutes or until heated through. Place remaining potatoes on a baking sheet. Freeze overnight or until thoroughly frozen; transfer to a freezer bag. May be frozen for up to 3 months.

To use frozen potatoes: Place the potatoes on a microwave-safe plate. Microwave, uncovered, at 50% power for 8-9 minutes or until heated through. **Yield:** 4 servings.

Editor's Note: This recipe was tested in a 1,100-watt microwave.

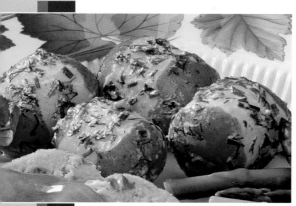

Herbed New Potatoes

Herbed
New Potatoes

Vi Neiding, South Milwaukee, Wisconsin

*I make these potatoes often for my husband
and me. They are easy to prepare and have a
nice dill flavor. We eagerly await the start of
farmers market season to get garden-fresh new
potatoes, especially for this recipe.*

- 3/4 **pound small red potatoes**
- 1 **tablespoon butter, softened**
- 1 **tablespoon sour cream**
- 2 **teaspoons snipped fresh dill** *or*
  1/2 teaspoon dill weed
- 2 **teaspoons minced chives**
- 1/4 **teaspoon salt**
- 1/8 **teaspoon pepper**

Dash lemon juice

Remove a strip of peel from the middle
of each potato. Place potatoes in a
saucepan and cover with water. Bring to
a boil over medium heat. Reduce heat;
cover and simmer for 20 minutes or
until potatoes are tender.

In a small bowl, combine the remaining ingredients. Drain potatoes;
add butter mixture and toss gently.
Yield: 2 servings.

Apple
Sweet Potato Bake

Opal Sanders, Glouster, Ohio

*Mother never used a recipe, so for years, there
were no written instructions to make this
bake. When the memories of this Thanksgiv-
ing side dish began to haunt me, I set out to
duplicate this favorite dish, which took me
many tries. It bakes in the oven with other
foods, needing little attention.*

- 5 **medium sweet potatoes (2-1/2
  pounds)**
- 4 **cups sliced peeled tart apples
  (about 4 medium)**
- 3/4 **cup apple juice concentrate**
- 1-1/2 **cups plus 2 tablespoons cold
  water,** *divided*
- 1/4 **cup sugar**
- 1/4 **cup packed brown sugar**
- 1/2 **teaspoon salt**
- 7-1/2 **teaspoons cornstarch**
- 1/4 **cup butter, cubed**

Place sweet potatoes in a large saucepan
or Dutch oven and cover with water.
Bring to a boil; cover and cook for 30-
45 minutes or until potatoes are tender.
Drain. When cool enough to handle, peel
and slice potatoes.

Place apples in a large saucepan
and cover with water. Cover and cook
apples over medium heat for 7-8 minutes or until crisp-tender; drain. Place
the apples and sweet potatoes in a
greased 2-1/2-qt. baking dish.

In a small saucepan, combine apple
juice concentrate, 1-1/2 cups water,
sugars and salt. Combine cornstarch
with remaining water until smooth;
gradually stir into apple juice concentrate mixture. Bring to a boil; cook and
stir mixture for 2 minutes or until thickened and bubbly.

Remove mixture from the heat; stir
in butter until melted. Pour over potato mixture. Bake, uncovered, at 325°
for 30-35 minutes or until heated
through. **Yield:** 12 servings.

Au Gratin
Garlic Potatoes

Tonya Vowels, Vine Grove, Kentucky

*Cream cheese and a can of cheese soup turn
these ordinary sliced potatoes into a rich side
that is a perfect accompaniment to almost any
main dish.*

- 1/2 **cup milk**
- 1 **can (10-3/4 ounces) condensed
  cheddar cheese soup, undiluted**
- 1 **package (8 ounces) cream
  cheese, cubed**
- 1 **garlic clove, minced**
- 1/4 **teaspoon ground nutmeg**
- 1/8 **teaspoon pepper**
- 2 **pounds potatoes, peeled and
  sliced**
- 1 **small onion, chopped**

Paprika, optional

In a saucepan, heat milk over medium
heat until bubbles form around side of
saucepan. Remove from the heat. Add
the soup, cream cheese, garlic, nutmeg
and pepper; stir until smooth.

Place the potatoes and onion in a 3-qt.
slow cooker. Pour the milk mixture over
the potato mixture; mix well.

Cover and cook on low for 6-7 hours
or until the potatoes are tender. Sprinkle with paprika if desired. **Yield:** 6-8
servings.

Apple Sweet Potato Bake

Zucchini Twice-Baked Potatoes

Swiss Scalloped Potatoes

Our Test Kitchen came up with this ultimate comfort food that even calorie-counters can feel comfortable eating. With a pleasant hint of rosemary and Swiss cheese, these down-home potatoes cook up tender and creamy.

- 9 cups sliced peeled potatoes (2-1/2 pounds)
- 4 cups 2% milk
- 2 teaspoons salt
- 1 garlic clove, minced
- 1/4 teaspoon white pepper
- 1 fresh rosemary sprig
- 1 bay leaf
- 4 teaspoons cornstarch
- 2 tablespoons cold water
- 4 ounces reduced-fat Swiss cheese, shredded
- 1-1/2 cups soft bread crumbs
- 2 tablespoons butter, melted

In a large saucepan or Dutch oven, combine the potatoes, milk, salt, garlic, pepper, rosemary sprig and bay leaf. Bring to a boil. Reduce heat to low; cover and cook for 6-8 minutes or until almost tender. Discard rosemary sprig and bay leaf.

In a small bowl, combine cornstarch and cold water until smooth; stir into potato mixture. Bring to a boil. Reduce heat; cook and stir for 2 minutes. Remove potato mixture from the heat; gently stir in cheese.

Transfer to a 13-in. x 9-in. x 2-in. baking dish coated with nonstick cooking spray. Combine bread crumbs and butter; sprinkle over potato mixture. Bake, uncovered, at 350° for 25-30 minutes or until bubbly and crumbs are golden brown. **Yield:** 12 servings.

Zucchini Twice-Baked Potatoes

Mary Maxeiner, Lakewood, Colorado

Flecks of zucchini add pretty color to these twice-baked potatoes. My mother prepared them each Christmas when I was young. Now years later, my brothers, sister and I rely on the recipe for any special family meal.

- 3 large baking potatoes (about 3/4 pound *each*)
- 3 cups shredded zucchini (about 2 medium)
- 1 medium onion, chopped
- 2 tablespoons butter, *divided*
- 1/2 cup sour cream
- 3/4 to 1 teaspoon salt
- 1/8 to 1/4 teaspoon pepper
- 1/2 cup shredded cheddar cheese

Scrub and pierce potatoes. Bake at 400° for 50-75 minutes or until the potatoes are tender. Cool until easy to handle. Reduce heat to 350°. In a large skillet, saute zucchini and onion in 1 tablespoon butter until tender. Drain and set aside.

Scoop out the potato pulp, leaving a thin shell; place the pulp in a bowl and mash. Add the sour cream, salt, pepper and remaining butter; mash. Stir in zucchini mixture. Spoon into the potato shells. Sprinkle with the cheese.

Place potatoes on a baking sheet. Bake at 20-25 minutes or until potatoes are heated through and the cheese is melted. **Yield:** 6 servings.

Golden Diced Potatoes

Angela Tiffany Wegerer, Colwich, Kansas

My aunt once made potatoes like these for us. When I couldn't remember her exact recipe, I created this version. The lightly seasoned coating on the potatoes cooks to a pretty golden brown and packs in a lot of flavor.

- 3/4 cup all-purpose flour
- 1 teaspoon seasoned salt
- 1/2 teaspoon onion powder
- 1/4 teaspoon garlic powder
- 1/4 teaspoon pepper
- 4 medium potatoes, peeled and cut into 1/2-inch pieces
- 1/2 cup butter

In a large resealable plastic bag, combine the first five ingredients. Add 1/2 cup potatoes at a time; shake to coat.

In two large skillets, melt butter. Add potatoes; cook and stir over medium heat for 25-30 minutes or until potatoes are tender. **Yield:** 6 servings.

Quick Tip

For an easy, change-of-pace potato topping, leave out the butter, sour cream and salt and try a little Ranch salad dressing. It's a no-stress, full-flavored way to dress up your spuds.

Golden Diced Potatoes

Mixed Grill Kabobs (p. 66)

Meat & Potato Lover's Cookbook

Chapter 4

Grilled Greats

Nothing tempts taste buds more than the sizzle and smoky flavor of food hot off the grill. Whether you're craving a thick, juicy burger or a mouth-watering steak, these meaty grilled favorites will fit the bill.

T-Bones with Onions

Hawaiian Honey Burgers

Sheryl Creech, Lancaster, California

These burgers were a favorite when I was growing up. I now use them as a way to "fancy up" a barbecue without a lot of extra preparation. Fresh fruit and corn on the cob are wonderful accompaniments.

- 2 **pounds ground beef**
- 1/2 **cup honey**
- 1/4 **teaspoon ground cinnamon**
- 1/4 **teaspoon paprika**
- 1/4 **teaspoon curry powder**
- 1/8 **teaspoon ground ginger**
- 1/8 **teaspoon ground nutmeg**
- 1/4 **cup soy sauce**
- 1 **can (20 ounces) sliced pineapple, drained**
- 8 **hamburger buns, split and toasted**

Lettuce leaves, optional

In a bowl, combine the first seven ingredients; mix well. Shape into eight 3/4-in.-thick patties. Grill the burgers, uncovered, over medium-hot heat for 3 minutes on each side. Brush with the soy sauce.

Continue grilling for 4-6 minutes or until juices run clear, basting and turning several times. During the last 4 minutes, grill the pineapple slices until browned, turning once. Serve burgers and pineapple on buns with lettuce if desired. **Yield:** 8 servings.

T-Bones with Onions

Sheree Quate, Cave Junction, Oregon

Steak gets a dressy treatment when topped with tasty onion slices flavored with honey and ground mustard. I found this recipe on a bag of charcoal more than 10 years ago. It's terrific with green beans or corn.

- 3 **large onions, cut into 1/4-inch-thick slices**
- 2 **tablespoons honey**
- 1/2 **teaspoon salt**
- 1/2 **teaspoon ground mustard**
- 1/2 **teaspoon paprika**
- 1/2 **teaspoon pepper**
- 4 **beef T-bone steaks (1 inch thick and 12 ounces *each*)**

Additional salt and pepper

Place onions in the center of a piece of heavy-duty foil (about 20 in. x 18 in.). Drizzle with honey; sprinkle with the salt, mustard, paprika and pepper. Fold foil over onions and seal tightly. Season steaks with additional salt and pepper.

Grill onions and steaks, covered, over medium heat. Grill onions for 10-12 minutes on each side or until tender. Grill steak for 7-10 minutes on each side or until meat reaches desired doneness (for medium-rare, a meat thermometer should read 145°; medium, 160°; well-done, 170°). Let steak stand for 3-5 minutes. Serve with onions. **Yield:** 4 servings.

Provolone Pepper Burgers

Nick Mescia, Surprise, Arizona

I'm known around the neighborhood as the "grill sergeant." I'm often seen making these tasty burgers on my built-in patio gas grill.

- 1/3 **cup finely cubed provolone cheese**
- 1/4 **cup diced roasted red peppers**
- 1/4 **cup finely chopped onion**

Salt and pepper to taste

- 1 **pound ground beef**
- 4 **hamburger buns, split**

In a bowl, combine the cheese, peppers, onion, salt and pepper. Add beef and mix well. Shape into four patties.

Grill, covered, over medium-hot heat for 4-5 minutes on each side or until meat is no longer pink. Serve on buns. **Yield:** 4 servings.

Quick Tip

Hamburgers make it a snap to mix up your dinnertime routine. For a tasty change, forget the bun. Slice up cooked patties and roll them in a tortillas or stuff them into a pita bread.

Hawaiian Honey Burgers

Tender Flank Steak

Barbecued Beef Short Ribs

Paula Zsiray, Logan, Utah

Sweet-spicy barbecue ribs are always a hit. The sauce is also very good on pork ribs.

- 1 cup sugar
- 1/2 cup packed brown sugar
- 2 tablespoons salt
- 2 tablespoons garlic powder
- 2 tablespoons paprika
- 2 teaspoons pepper
- 1/4 teaspoon cayenne pepper
- 7 pounds bone-in beef short ribs

SAUCE

- 1 small onion, finely chopped
- 2 teaspoons vegetable oil
- 1-1/2 cups water
- 1 cup ketchup
- 1 can (6 ounces) tomato paste
- 2 tablespoons brown sugar

Pepper to taste

In a bowl, combine the first seven ingredients; rub over ribs. Place in two large resealable plastic bags; seal and refrigerate overnight.

Line two 15-in. x 10-in. x 1-in. baking pans with foil; grease the foil. Place ribs in prepared pans. Bake, uncovered, at 325° for 2 hours or until meat is tender.

Meanwhile, in a large saucepan, saute onion in oil until tender. Stir in the water, ketchup, tomato paste, brown sugar and pepper. Bring to a boil. Reduce heat; cover and simmer for 1 hour.

Remove ribs from the oven. Grill ribs, covered, over indirect medium heat for 20 minutes, turning and basting frequently with sauce. **Yield:** 14 servings.

Barbecued Beef Short Ribs

Tender Flank Steak

Gayle Bucknam, Greenbank, Washington

This mildly marinated flank steak is my son's favorite. I usually slice it thinly and serve it with twice-baked potatoes and a green salad to round out the meal. Leftovers are great for French dip sandwiches.

✓ *Uses less fat, sugar or salt. Includes Nutrition Facts and Diabetic Exchanges.*

- 1/4 cup soy sauce
- 2 tablespoons water
- 3 garlic cloves, thinly sliced
- 1 tablespoon brown sugar
- 1 tablespoon vegetable oil
- 1/2 teaspoon ground ginger
- 1/2 teaspoon pepper
- 1 flank steak (1 pound)

In a large resealable plastic bag or shallow glass container, combine the first seven ingredients; mix well. Add steak and turn to coat. Cover and refrigerate for 8 hours or overnight, turning occasionally.

Drain and discard marinade. Grill, covered, over medium-hot heat for 6-8 minutes on each side or until meat reaches desired doneness (for medium-rare, a meat thermometer should read 145°; medium, 160°; well-done, 170°). **Yield:** 4 servings.

Nutrition Facts: 1 serving (prepared with reduced-sodium soy sauce) equals 209 calories, 11 g fat (0 saturated fat), 59 mg cholesterol, 326 mg sodium, 3 g carbohydrate, trace fiber, 24 g protein. **Diabetic Exchange:** 3-1/2 lean meat.

Peppery Grilled Steaks

Lynn McAllister, Mt. Ulla, North Carolina

Coarsely ground pepper adds the perfect amount of spice to flank steaks. We enjoy this grilled entree year-round.

- 1/4 cup red wine vinegar
- 1/4 cup olive oil
- 1/4 cup Dijon mustard
- 4 garlic cloves, minced
- 2 green onions, chopped
- 4 teaspoons coarsely ground pepper
- 1 teaspoon dried thyme
- 1 teaspoon dried rosemary, crushed
- 1/2 teaspoon salt
- 3 beef flank steaks (about 1 pound *each*)

In a large resealable plastic bag, combine vinegar, oil, mustard, garlic, onions, pepper, thyme, rosemary and salt; add steaks. Seal bag and turn to coat; refrigerate for 8 hours or overnight.

Drain and discard marinade. Grill steaks, covered, over medium heat for 6-10 minutes on each side or until meat reaches desired doneness (for medium-rare, a meat thermometer should read 145°; medium, 160°; well-done, 170°). **Yield:** 10-12 servings.

Sirloin Squash Shish Kabobs

Ronda Karbo, Russell, Minnesota

When our grill comes out in the spring, this is the first recipe my family asks me to make. You can also use this marinade on six pork chops or a large piece of round steak cut into serving-size pieces.

- 1 **cup packed brown sugar**
- 1 **cup soy sauce**
- 1 **teaspoon** *each* **garlic powder, ground mustard and ground ginger**
- 1 **pound boneless beef sirloin steak, cut into 1-inch pieces**
- 1 **medium zucchini, cut into 1/4-inch slices**
- 1 **medium yellow summer squash, cut into 1/4-inch slices**
- 1 **medium sweet red pepper, cut into 1-inch pieces**
- 1 **medium red onion, cut into eight wedges, optional**

In a small bowl, combine the brown sugar, soy sauce, garlic powder, mustard and ginger. Place beef in a large resealable plastic bag; add 1 cup marinade. Seal bag and toss to coat. Place zucchini, yellow squash, red pepper and onion if desired in another resealable plastic bag; add remaining marinade and toss to coat. Refrigerate beef and vegetables for at least 4 hours, turning occasionally.

Drain and discard marinade. On eight metal or soaked wooden skewers, alternately thread beef and vegetables. Grill, covered, over medium-hot heat or broil 4-6 in. from the heat for 10 minutes or until meat reaches desired doneness, turning occasionally. **Yield:** 4 servings.

Marinated Sirloin Steak

Corina Flansberg, Carson City, Nevada

This recipe was given to me by a dear friend who knows that I like to grill. No one ever guesses that the secret ingredient is lemon-lime soda. Try the marinade with chicken, too. It's just wonderful!

- 1 **cup lemon-lime soda**
- 3/4 **cup vegetable oil**
- 3/4 **cup soy sauce**
- 1/4 **cup lemon juice**
- 1 **teaspoon garlic powder**
- 1 **teaspoon prepared horseradish**
- 1 **boneless beef sirloin steak (about 1 pound)**

In a large resealable plastic bag, combine the first six ingredients. Add steak and turn to coat. Seal and refrigerate 8 hours or overnight, turning occasionally.

Drain and discard marinade. Grill steaks, covered, over medium-hot heat for 3-5 minutes on each side or until meat reaches desired doneness (for medium-rare, a meat thermometer should read 145°; medium, 160°; well-done, 170°). **Yield:** 4 servings.

Sirloin Squash Shish Kabobs

Garlic-Pepper Tenderloin Steaks

Vicki Atkinson, Kamas, Utah

I give a little kick to these grilled tenderloin steaks with a zippy dry rub that combines paprika, thyme, ground mustard, chili powder and cayenne pepper. The steaks can also be broiled when the weather isn't quite right for grilling.

✓ *Uses less fat, sugar or salt. Includes Nutrition Facts and Diabetic Exchanges.*

- 1-1/2 **teaspoons minced garlic**
- 1 **teaspoon ground mustard**
- 1 **teaspoon paprika**
- 1 **teaspoon chili powder**
- 1 **teaspoon pepper**
- 1/2 **teaspoon salt**
- 1/2 **teaspoon dried thyme**
- 1/4 **to 1/2 teaspoon cayenne pepper**
- 4 **beef tenderloin steaks (4 ounces each)**
- 2 **teaspoons olive oil**

In a small bowl, combine the seasonings. Brush steaks with oil; rub in seasoning mixture. Cover and refrigerate for at least 1 hour.

If grilling the steaks, coat grill rack with nonstick cooking spray before starting the grill. Grill steaks, uncovered, over medium heat or broil 4-6 in. from the heat for 7-10 minutes on each side or until meat reaches desired doneness (for medium-rare, a meat thermometer should read 145°; medium, 160°; well-done, 170°). **Yield:** 4 servings.

Nutrition Facts: 1 serving (3 ounces cooked beef) equals 209 calories, 11 g fat (3 g saturated fat), 70 mg cholesterol, 353 mg sodium, 2 g carbohydrate, 1 g fiber, 24 g protein. **Diabetic Exchanges:** 3 lean meat, 1/2 fat.

Quick Tip

One way to prepare kabobs is to assemble each skewer so it features one type of food. Remove each kabob from the heat when done cooking, combine all of the grilled food into one large serving bowl.

Barbecued Burgers

Rhoda Troyer, Glenford, Ohio

I can't take all the credit for these winning burgers. My husband's uncle passed down the special barbecue sauce recipe. We love it on everything, so it was only natural to try it with these burgers.

SAUCE

- 1 cup ketchup
- 1/2 cup packed brown sugar
- 1/3 cup sugar
- 1/4 cup honey
- 1/4 cup molasses
- 2 teaspoons prepared mustard
- 1-1/2 teaspoons Worcestershire sauce
- 1/4 teaspoon salt
- 1/4 teaspoon Liquid Smoke
- 1/8 teaspoon pepper

BURGERS

- 1 egg, beaten
- 1/3 cup quick-cooking oats
- 1/4 teaspoon onion salt
- 1/4 teaspoon garlic salt
- 1/4 teaspoon pepper
- 1/8 teaspoon salt
- 1-1/2 pounds ground beef
- 6 hamburger buns, split

Toppings of your choice

In a small saucepan, combine the first 10 ingredients. Bring to a boil. Remove from the heat. Set aside 1 cup barbecue sauce to serve with burgers.

In a bowl, combine the egg, oats, 1/4 cup of the remaining barbecue sauce, onion salt, garlic salt, pepper and salt. Crumble beef over mixture; mix well. Shape into six patties.

Grill, covered, over medium heat for 6-8 minutes on each side or until a meat thermometer reads 160°, basting with 1/2 cup barbecue sauce during the last 5 minutes. Serve on buns with toppings of your choice and reserved barbecue sauce. **Yield:** 6 servings.

Grilled Vegetable Potato Skins

Karen Hemminger, Mansfield, Massachusetts

People just love these stuffed spuds in the summer as an alternative to heavier grilled fare. Topped with a colorful vegetable medley, the tender potato skins are light yet satisfying.

- 2 large baking potatoes
- 1 cup sliced yellow summer squash
- 1 cup sliced zucchini
- 1/2 large sweet red pepper, julienned
- 1/2 large green pepper, julienned
- 1 small red onion, cut into 1/4-inch wedges
- 1/4 cup reduced-fat Italian salad dressing
- 1-1/2 teaspoons olive oil
- 1/2 teaspoon salt, *divided*
- 1/4 cup shredded reduced-fat cheddar cheese

Pierce potatoes several times with a fork and place on a microwave-safe plate. Microwave on high for 18-20 minutes or until tender, rotating the potatoes once. Let stand until cool enough to handle.

Meanwhile, in a large resealable plastic bag, combine the summer squash, zucchini, peppers and onion. Pour salad dressing over vegetables. Seal bag and turn to coat; marinate for 20 minutes.

Cut each potato in half lengthwise. Scoop out pulp, leaving a thin shell (discard pulp or save for another use). Brush inside of shells with oil and sprinkle with 1/4 teaspoon salt.

Coat grill rack with nonstick cooking spray. Place potato shells skin side up on grill rack. Grill, covered, over indirect medium heat for 10 minutes or until golden brown.

Drain vegetables, reserving marinade. Grill vegetables in a grill basket, uncovered, over medium heat for 10 minutes or until tender, basting with reserved marinade.

Sprinkle potato skins with cheese. Fill with grilled vegetables; sprinkle with remaining salt. Grill 5 minutes longer or until cheese is melted. **Yield:** 4 servings.

Editor's Note: This recipe was tested with an 850-watt microwave.

Grilled Vegetable Potato Skins

Meal on a Stick

Sundra Hauck, Bogalusa, Louisiana

My husband and I were thrilled to receive a gas grill as a wedding gift from some church friends. We love to grill these hearty meatball-and-veggie kabobs. Barbecue sauce gives them a slightly sweet flavor. Olives are a fun addition.

- 8 **small red potatoes**
- 2 **eggs, lightly beaten**
- 2 **teaspoons Worcestershire sauce**
- 1-1/4 **cups seasoned bread crumbs**
- 1 **teaspoon curry powder**
- 1-1/2 **pounds ground beef**
- 24 **stuffed olives**
- 8 **plum tomatoes, halved**
- 2 **medium green peppers, cut into quarters**
- 8 **large fresh mushrooms**
- 1/4 **cup barbecue sauce**

Scrub and pierce potatoes; place on a microwave-safe plate. Microwave, uncovered, on high for 3-5 minutes or until slightly tender.

Meanwhile, in a large bowl, combine the eggs, Worcestershire sauce, bread crumbs and curry powder. Crumble beef over mixture and mix well. Divide into 24 portions; shape each portion around an olive. Alternately thread meatballs and vegetables onto metal or soaked wooden skewers.

Grill kabobs, covered, over medium hot heat for 5 minutes. Turn; brush with barbecue sauce. Cook 5 minutes longer or until meatballs are no longer pink, basting once. **Yield:** 6-8 servings.

Editor's Note: This recipe was tested in a 1,100-watt microwave.

Italian Flank Steak

Walajean Saglett, Canandaigua, New York

Savory and satisfying, this recipe is nice for entertaining or busy days since the steak marinates overnight and grills in minutes. Leftovers—if there are any—make super sandwiches for lunch.

✔ *Uses less fat, sugar or salt. Includes Nutrition Facts and Diabetic Exchanges.*

- 2 **envelopes (.7 ounce *each*) fat-free Italian salad dressing mix**
- 2 **tablespoons vegetable oil**
- 1 **tablespoon lemon juice**
- 1 **beef flank steak (1 pound)**

Combine salad dressing mix, oil and lemon juice. Brush onto both sides of steak; place in a shallow dish. Cover and refrigerate several hours or overnight.

Grill over hot heat for 4 minutes per side for medium, 5 minutes per side for medium-well or until desired doneness is reached. **Yield:** 4 servings.

Nutrition Facts: 1 serving (4 ounces) equals 267 calories, 16 g fat (0 saturated fat), 59 mg cholesterol, 793 mg sodium, 8 g carbohydrate, 0 fiber, 24 g protein. **Diabetic Exchanges:** 3 meat, 1/2 starch.

Thyme Lemon Sirloins

Suzanne Whitaker, Knoxville, Tennessee

We love to serve steaks when friends drop by...and have found that the tangy lemon-herb rub in this recipe really livens up the taste buds.

- 2 **teaspoons grated lemon peel**
- 2 **garlic cloves, minced**
- 1 **teaspoon dried thyme**
- 1/4 **teaspoon salt**
- 1/4 **teaspoon pepper**
- 2 **tablespoons butter**
- 1 **tablespoons lemon juice**
- 4 **boneless beef sirloin steaks (about 2 pounds and 1 inch thick)**

In a small bowl, combine the lemon peel, garlic, thyme, salt and pepper. Set aside 1 tablespoon seasoning mixture for steaks. In a small saucepan, melt butter; stir in lemon juice and remaining seasoning mixture. Set aside and keep warm.

Rub steaks with reserved seasoning mixture. Grill steaks, uncovered, over medium heat for 8-12 minutes on each side or until meat reaches desired doneness (for medium-rare, a meat thermometer should read 145°; medium, 160°; well-done, 170°). Serve with reserved butter sauce. **Yield:** 4 servings.

Meal on a Stick

Decked-Out Burgers

Cool-Kitchen Meat Loaf

Susan Taul, Birmingham, Alabama

Juicy slices of this tender meat loaf are wonderful served with a homemade sweet-and-sour sauce. It's an easy way to fix supper.

- 1 cup soft bread crumbs
- 1 medium onion, chopped
- 1/2 cup tomato sauce
- 1 egg
- 1-1/2 teaspoons salt
- 1/4 teaspoon pepper
- 1-1/2 pounds lean ground beef

SAUCE

- 1/2 cup ketchup
- 3 tablespoons brown sugar
- 3 tablespoons Worcestershire sauce
- 2 tablespoons vinegar
- 2 tablespoons prepared mustard

In a bowl, combine the first six ingredients. Add beef and mix well. Shape into two loaves; place each loaf in a disposable 8-in. x 4-in. x 2-in. loaf pan. Cover with foil. Grill, covered, over indirect medium heat for 30 minutes or until the meat is no longer pink and a meat thermometer reads 160°.

Meanwhile, in a saucepan, combine the sauce ingredients. Cook and stir over low heat until sugar is dissolved. Spoon over meat loaves before serving. **Yield:** 2 loaves (3 servings each).

Decked-Out Burgers

Karen Bourne, Magrath, Alberta

Guests will enjoy this burger's topping of bacon, cheese, mushrooms and mayonnaise.

- 1 cup (4 ounces) shredded cheddar cheese
- 1 jar (4-1/2 ounces) sliced mushrooms, drained
- 1/3 cup mayonnaise
- 6 bacon strips, cooked and crumbled
- 1-1/2 pounds lean ground beef
- 1/4 cup finely chopped onion
- 1 teaspoon salt
- 1/2 teaspoon pepper
- 1/4 teaspoon garlic powder
- 1/8 teaspoon hot pepper sauce
- 6 hamburger buns, split

Lettuce leaves and tomato slices, optional

In a bowl, combine cheese, mushrooms, mayonnaise and bacon; cover and refrigerate. In another bowl, combine the beef, onion, salt, pepper, garlic powder and hot pepper sauce. Shape into six 1/2-in.-thick patties.

Grill, covered, over medium-hot heat for 4-5 minutes on each side. Spoon cheese mixture on top of each burger. Grill 1-2 minutes longer or until the cheese begins to melt. Serve on buns with lettuce and tomato if desired. **Yield:** 6 servings.

Honey-Mustard Beef Kabobs

Suzanne McKinley, Lyons, Georgia

Here's an easy entree that's sure to get mustard lovers all fired up. I rely on the tangy condiment to season these beefy skewers. Serve kabobs with a fast side dish of white rice.

- 1/2 cup Dijon mustard
- 1/4 cup honey
- 1 teaspoon Worcestershire sauce
- 1/4 teaspoon salt
- 1/8 teaspoon pepper
- 3/4 pound boneless beef sirloin steak, cut into 1-inch cubes

In a bowl, combine the mustard, honey, Worcestershire sauce, salt and pepper. Pour half of the sauce into a large resealable plastic bag; add beef cubes and toss to coat. Set the remaining sauce aside.

Thread beef onto metal or soaked wooden skewers. Discard marinade from beef. Grill, covered, over medium heat for 8-10 minutes or until meat reaches desired doneness, turning once. Serve with reserved sauce. **Yield:** 3 servings.

Cool-Kitchen Meat Loaf

Mixed Grill Kabobs

Mixed Grill Kabobs

Glenda Adams, Vanndale, Arkansas

These hearty kabobs combine beef and sausage, two of my favorite foods. Both the meat and vegetables are marinated before they're grilled, which makes this skewered meal extra flavorful. Be sure to fire up your grill and try these soon!

- **3 cups pineapple juice**
- **1 cup cider vinegar**
- **1 cup vegetable oil**
- **1/4 cup sugar**
- **1/4 cup soy sauce**
- **1 tablespoon browning sauce, optional**
- **1/2 teaspoon garlic powder**
- **1/4 teaspoon lemon-pepper seasoning**
- **2 pounds beef tenderloin, cut into 1-inch cubes**
- **1 pound smoked kielbasa *or* Polish sausage, cut into 1-inch chunks**
- **3 to 4 medium tomatoes, quartered**
- **3 to 4 medium green peppers, quartered**
- **1 jar (4-1/2 ounces) whole mushrooms, drained**
- **5 medium onions, quartered**

In a large resealable plastic bag, combine the first eight ingredients. Add the meat and vegetables. Seal bag and turn to coat; refrigerate overnight.

Drain and discard marinade. Alternately thread beef, sausage and vegetable onto metal or soaked wooden skewers. Grill, covered, over medium-hot heat for 6-8 minutes. Turn kabobs; cook 6-8 minutes longer or until beef reaches desired doneness. **Yield:** 10-12 servings.

Steak and Potato Salad

Linda Emily Dow
Princeton Junction, New Jersey

I like to spend a lot of time with our family and friends on weekends. That's when this meal-and-potatoes recipe comes in handy. We grill it quickly for a fast, filling meal.

- **2 pounds boneless sirloin steak (1 inch thick)**
- **1/2 cup cider *or* red wine vinegar**
- **1/4 cup olive *or* vegetable oil**
- **1/4 cup soy sauce**
- **6 cups cubed cooked potatoes**
- **1 cup diced green pepper**
- **1/3 cup chopped green onions**
- **1/4 cup minced fresh parsley**
- **1/2 cup Caesar salad dressing**

Lettuce leaves, optional

Place steak in a large resealable plastic bag or shallow glass container. Combine vinegar, oil and soy sauce; pour over the steak. Cover and refrigerate for 1 hour or overnight. Drain, discarding marinade. Grill or broil steak for 8-10 minutes on each side or until meat reaches desired doneness (for medium-rare, a meat thermometer should read 145°; medium, 160°; well-done, 170°).

Slice into thin strips across grain and place in a bowl. Add potatoes, green peppers, onions, parsley and dressing; toss to coat. Serve on lettuce if desired. **Yield:** 9 servings.

Robust Marinated Steak

Betty Ann Ewert, Arlington, Minnesota

Anytime is a good time to fire up the grill and toss on a steak that's soaked up this great marinade. One of our stock-car-racing buddies came up with the recipe, and we use it all the time.

✓ *Uses less fat, sugar or salt. Includes Nutrition Facts.*

- **2 tablespoons red wine vinegar**
- **2 tablespoons pineapple juice**
- **4-1/2 teaspoons brown sugar**
- **1 tablespoon Liquid Smoke**
- **1-1/2 teaspoons soy sauce**
- **1/2 teaspoon salt**
- **1/4 teaspoon onion powder**
- **1/8 teaspoon pepper**
- **1 garlic clove, minced**
- **3/4 pound boneless beef sirloin steak (1 inch thick)**

In a large resealable plastic bag, combine the first nine ingredients; add steak. Seal bag and turn to coat; refrigerate overnight.

Drain and discard marinade. Grill steak, uncovered, over medium heat for 4-8 minutes on each side or until meat reaches desired doneness (for medium-rare, a meat thermometer should read 145°; medium, 160°; well-done, 170°). **Yield:** 2 servings.

Nutrition Facts: 1 serving equals 267 calories, 8 g fat (3 g saturated fat), 95 mg cholesterol, 896 mg sodium, 14 g carbohydrate, trace fiber, 33 g protein.

Robust Marinated Steak

All-American Hamburgers

steak. Seal bag and turn to coat; refrigerate for 3 hours or overnight, turning occasionally.

Coat grill rack with nonstick cooking spray before starting the grill. Drain and discard marinade. Grill steak, covered, over medium-hot heat for 6-8 minutes on each side or until meat reaches desired doneness (for medium-rare, a meat thermometer should read 145°; medium, 160°, well-done, 170°). **Yield:** 6 servings.

Nutrition Facts: 1 serving (3 ounces cooked beef) equals 200 calories, 10 g fat (4 g saturated fat), 59 mg cholesterol, 253 mg sodium, 3 g carbohydrate, trace fiber, 24 g protein. **Diabetic Exchange:** 3 lean meat.

Grilled Hash Browns

Kelly Chastain, Bedford, Indiana

Since my husband and I love to grill meats, we're always looking for easy side dishes that cook on the grill, too. That's why I came up with this simple recipe for hash browns.

- 3-1/2 **cups frozen cubed hash brown potatoes, thawed**
- 1 **small onion, chopped**
- 1 **tablespoon beef bouillon granules**

Dash **seasoned salt**

Dash **pepper**

- 1 **tablespoon butter, melted**

Place potatoes on a piece of heavy-duty foil (about 20 in. x 18 in.) coated with nonstick cooking spray. Sprinkle with onion, bouillon, seasoned salt and pepper; drizzle with butter.

Fold foil around potatoes and seal tightly. Grill, covered, over indirect medium heat for 10-15 minutes or until potatoes are tender, turning once. **Yield:** 4 servings.

All-American Hamburgers

Diane Hixon, Niceville, Florida

We do a lot of camping and outdoor cooking. Hamburgers are on our menu more than any other food.

- 2 **tablespoons diced onion**
- 2 **tablespoons chili sauce**
- 2 **teaspoons Worcestershire sauce**
- 2 **teaspoons prepared mustard**
- 1 **pound ground beef**
- 4 **slices American** *or* **cheddar cheese, halved diagonally**
- 2 **slices Swiss cheese, halved diagonally**
- 4 **hamburger buns, split and toasted**

Lettuce leaves, sliced tomato and onion, cooked bacon, ketchup and mustard, optional

In a bowl, combine the first four ingredients. Crumble beef over mixture and mix well. Shape into four patties.

Grill, covered, over medium heat for 6 minutes on each side or until meat is no longer pink. During the last minute of cooking, top each patty with two triangles of American cheese and one triangle of Swiss cheese. Serve on buns with lettuce, tomato, onion, bacon, ketchup and mustard if desired. **Yield:** 4 servings.

Paprika Chili Steak

Diann Mallehan, Grand Rapids, Michigan

Marinate seasoned with chili powder and paprika gives grilled flank steak a robust flavor. This treasured dish is from a neighbor.

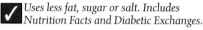 *Uses less fat, sugar or salt. Includes Nutrition Facts and Diabetic Exchanges.*

- 1 **medium onion, chopped**
- 1/2 **cup ketchup**
- 1/4 **cup cider vinegar**
- 1 **tablespoon paprika**
- 1 **tablespoon canola oil**
- 2 **teaspoons chili powder**
- 1 **teaspoon salt**
- 1/8 **teaspoon pepper**
- 1-1/2 **pounds beef flank steak**

In a large resealable plastic bag, combine the first eight ingredients; add

Paprika Chili Steak

a cheese slice on each patty; cover and grill until cheese is melted. Layer bottom half of each bun with lettuce, patty, bacon and mayonnaise mixture. Add bun tops. **Yield:** 8 servings.

Dressed-Up Bacon Burgers

Dressed-Up Bacon Burgers

Carol Mizell, Ruston, Louisiana

The tangy, homemade sauce that tops these mouth-watering burgers helps them stand out from the rest. Because the bacon cooks on the grill alongside the burgers, cleanup is a breeze, too.

- 3/4 **cup mayonnaise**
- 3 **tablespoons sweet pickle relish**
- 3 **tablespoons ketchup**
- 1 **tablespoon sugar**
- 1 **tablespoon dried minced onion**
- 1 **tablespoon Worcestershire sauce**
- 1/2 **teaspoon salt**
- 1/4 **teaspoon garlic powder**
- 1/4 **teaspoon pepper**
- 2 **pounds ground beef**
- 8 **bacon strips**
- 8 **slices cheddar cheese**
- 8 **hamburger buns, split and toasted**

Lettuce leaves

In a small bowl, whisk the mayonnaise, pickle relish, ketchup, sugar and onion until well blended. Cover and refrigerate. In a large bowl, combine the Worcestershire sauce, salt, garlic powder and pepper. Crumble the beef over mixture; mix well. Shape into eight patties.

Place bacon on a piece of heavy-duty foil on one side of the grill. Place the patties on the other side of the grill. Grill, covered, over medium-hot heat for 20 minutes or until bacon is crisp and meat patties are no longer pink, turning once.

Drain bacon on paper towels. Place

Honey Barbecued Ribs

Joyce Duff, Mansfield, Ohio

My family celebrates four birthdays in July, and these tender ribs are a must at our joint get-together. Honey adds wonderful flavor to the homemade sauce.

- 3 **pounds country-style pork ribs**
- 1/2 **teaspoon garlic salt**
- 1/2 **teaspoon pepper**
- 1 **cup ketchup**
- 1/2 **cup packed brown sugar**
- 1/2 **cup honey**
- 1/4 **cup spicy brown mustard**
- 2 **tablespoons Worcestershire sauce**
- 1-1/2 **teaspoons Liquid Smoke, optional**

Place ribs in a large kettle or Dutch oven; sprinkle with garlic salt and pepper. Add enough water to cover; bring to a boil. Reduce heat; cover and simmer for 1 hour or until juices run clear and ribs are tender; drain.

Meanwhile, combine the remaining ingredients. Grill ribs, uncovered, over medium heat for 10-12 minutes, basting with sauce and turning occasionally. **Yield:** 4 servings.

Bacon-Wrapped Beef Patties

Jody Bahler, Wolcott, Indiana

My family loves these spruced-up hamburgers all year long. We think that the bacon, ketchup and Worcestershire sauce flavor the sandwiches and add a tasty twist. These pleasing patties can also be enjoyed off the bun. Give them a try tonight!

- 1 **cup (4 ounces) shredded cheddar cheese**
- 2/3 **cup chopped onion**
- 1/4 **cup ketchup**
- 2 **eggs, lightly beaten**
- 3 **tablespoons Worcestershire sauce**
- 2 **tablespoons grated Parmesan cheese**
- 1 **teaspoon seasoned salt**
- 1/4 **teaspoon pepper**
- 2 **pounds ground beef**
- 10 **bacon strips**
- 10 **hamburger buns, split, optional**

In a large bowl, combine the first eight ingredients. Crumble beef over mixture and mix well. Shape into ten 3/4-in.-thick patties. Wrap each patty with a bacon strip; secure with toothpicks.

Grill patties, uncovered, over medium heat for 5-6 minutes on each side or until juices run clear and a meat thermometer reads 160°. Serve on buns if desired. **Yield:** 10 servings.

Honey Barbecued Ribs

Steaks with Chipotle Sauce

Fillets with Mushroom Sauce

Carolyn Brinkmeyer, Aurora, Colorado

Grilled tenderloin steaks get an extra special treatment with the onion, mushrooms and tomatoes in this recipe. The sauce can be whipped up while the meat is on the grill for a special and quick main dish.

✓ *Uses less fat, sugar or salt. Includes Nutrition Facts and Diabetic Exchanges.*

- 4 **beef tenderloin fillets (4 ounces each)**
- 1 **large onion, cut into 1/2-inch slices**
- 1/2 **pound fresh mushrooms, thickly sliced**
- 2 **tablespoons butter**
- 1 **can (14-1/2 ounces) diced tomatoes, undrained**
- 1/4 **cup water**
- 1/2 **teaspoon dried basil**
- 1/2 **teaspoon beef bouillon granules**
- 1/8 **teaspoon pepper**

Grill fillets, covered, over medium heat for 6-9 minutes on each side or until meat reaches desired doneness (for medium-rare, a meat thermometer should read 145°; medium, 160°; well-done, 170°).

Meanwhile, in a large skillet, saute onion and mushrooms in butter until tender. Stir in the tomatoes, water, basil, bouillon and pepper. Bring to a boil; cook and stir over medium heat for 5 minutes or until thickened. Serve with beef. **Yield:** 4 servings.

Nutrition Facts: 1 fillet equals 278 calories, 14 g fat (0 saturated fat), 70 mg cholesterol, 299 mg sodium, 10 g carbohydrate, 0 fiber, 26 g protein. **Diabetic Exchanges:** 3 meat, 2 vegetable.

Teriyaki Beef Kabobs

Steaks with Chipotle Sauce

Canned chipotle peppers in adobo sauce make the perfect seasoning for this steak condiment. Try the no-stress, four-ingredient main course, or simply prepare the sauce and spread it over grilled chicken. It even perks up burgers and deli-meat sandwiches.

- 1 **can (7 ounces) chipotle peppers in adobo sauce**
- 1/2 **cup sour cream**
- 1 **teaspoon dried cilantro flakes**
- 4 **New York strip steaks (8 ounces each)**

Chop one chipotle pepper; place in a bowl. Add 1 teaspoon of the adobo sauce. Stir in sour cream and cilantro; refrigerate. (Save remaining peppers and sauce for another use.)

Grill steaks, uncovered, over medium-hot heat for 6-10 minutes on each side or until meat reaches desired doneness (for medium-rare, a meat thermometer should read 145°; medium, 160°; well-done, 170°). Serve with sauce. **Yield:** 4 servings.

Editor's Note: When cutting or seeding hot peppers, use rubber or plastic gloves to protect your hands. Avoid touching your face.

Quick Tip

Chipotles in adobo sauce are dried smoked red jalapeno peppers that are canned with a thick chili puree called adobo. Find them in the Mexican section of your supermarket.

Teriyaki Beef Kabobs

Lisa Hector, Estevan, Saskatchewan

My sister-in-law brought this recipe on a family camping trip and we fixed it for an outdoor potluck. It was so delicious that I asked for a copy to take home.

- 1/4 **cup vegetable oil**
- 1/4 **cup orange juice**
- 1/4 **cup soy sauce**
- 1 **teaspoon garlic powder**
- 1 **teaspoon ground ginger**
- 1-3/4 **pounds beef tenderloin, cut into 1-inch cubes**
- 3/4 **pound cherry tomatoes**
- 1/2 **pound whole fresh mushrooms**
- 2 **large green peppers, cubed**
- 1 **large red onion, cut into wedges**

Hot cooked rice, optional

In a resealable plastic bag or shallow glass container, combine the first five ingredients and mix well. Reserve 1/2 cup for basting and refrigerate. Add beef to remaining marinade; turn to coat. Seal bag or cover container; refrigerate for 1 hour, turning occasionally.

Drain and discard the marinade. On metal or soaked bamboo skewers, alternate beef, tomatoes, mushrooms, green peppers and onions. Grill, uncovered, over medium heat for 3 minutes on each side. Baste with reserved marinade. Continue turning and basting for 8-10 minutes or until meat reaches desired doneness (for medium-rare, a meat thermometer should read 145°; medium, 160°; well-done, 170°). Serve meat and vegetables over rice if desired. **Yield:** 6-8 servings.

Spicy Filet Mignon

Grilled Vegetable Medley

Susan Hase, Larsen, Wisconsin

Here's a hearty potato dish that's a no-fuss favorite of mine. And because everything is wrapped in foil and cooked on the grill, cleanup is a snap.

12	small red potatoes, halved
1	medium sweet potato, peeled and cut into chunks
4	tablespoons butter, melted, *divided*
4	to 6 garlic cloves, minced, *divided*
2	tablespoons minced fresh parsley, *divided*
1-1/2	teaspoons salt, *divided*
1/2	teaspoon lemon-pepper seasoning, *divided*
3/4	pound whole fresh mushrooms
1	large onion, sliced
1	medium green pepper, cut into 1/4-inch slices
1	small zucchini, cut into chunks
1	medium yellow summer squash, cut into chunks
1	cup (4 ounces) shredded part-skim mozzarella cheese *or* shredded Swiss cheese

Sour cream, optional

Place potatoes and sweet potato on an 18-in. x 15-in. piece of heavy-duty foil. Drizzle with half of the garlic, parsley, salt and lemon-pepper. Seal packet tightly. Grill, covered, over indirect medium-hot heat for 20 minutes on each side.

Meanwhile, place mushrooms, onion, green pepper, zucchini and summer squash on a 20-in. x 18-in. piece of heavy-duty foil. Drizzle with remaining butter; sprinkle with remaining seasonings. Seal packet tightly. Grill, covered, over medium-hot heat for 10 minutes on each side or until the vegetables are crisp-tender.

Combine the contents of both packets in a serving bowl; sprinkle with cheese. Serve with sour cream if desired. **Yield:** 8-10 servings.

Giant Mushroom Burger

Janice Delagrange, Mt. Airy, Maryland

I add mushrooms and onion to well-seasoned lean ground beef before forming it into one giant, family-pleasing patty. After grilling it, all I need to do is slice and serve.

✓ *Uses less fat, sugar or salt. Includes Nutrition Facts and Diabetic Exchanges.*

1-1/2	pounds lean ground beef
1	can (4 ounces) mushroom stems and pieces, drained
1/4	cup egg substitute
1/2	cup chopped onion
1/4	cup ketchup
1	teaspoon Italian seasoning
1	teaspoon fennel seed, crushed
1/4	teaspoon pepper
1/4	teaspoon Worcestershire sauce

Grilled Vegetable Medley

In a bowl, combine all ingredients. Pat into a 9-in. circle on a large sheet of waxed paper. Invert onto a greased wire grill basket; peel off waxed paper. Grill, covered, over medium heat for 20-25 minutes or until meat is no longer pink, turning once. Cut into six wedges. **Yield:** 6 servings.

Nutrition Facts: 1 serving equals 224 calories, 11 g fat (4 g saturated fat), 41 mg cholesterol, 305 mg sodium, 6 g carbohydrate, 1 g fiber, 25 g protein. **Diabetic Exchanges:** 3 lean meat, 1 vegetable.

Spicy Filet Mignon

Vera Kobiako, Jupiter, Florida

I adapted this recipe from a seasoning I saw for blackened catfish. Because these steaks have a lot of kick, I make a mild side dish, such as buttered potatoes, corn or grilled fresh vegetables.

2	tablespoons paprika
2	teaspoons onion salt
1-1/2	teaspoons garlic powder
1-1/2	teaspoons dried basil
1	to 1-1/2 teaspoons cayenne pepper
1	teaspoon dried thyme
6	beef tenderloin steaks (about 1-1/2 inches thick *each*)

Combine the seasonings; rub over steaks. Grill, covered, over indirect medium heat for 9-11 minutes on each side or until meat reaches desired doneness (for medium-rare, a meat thermometer should read 145°; medium, 160°; well-done, 170°). **Yield:** 6 servings.

Grilled Beef Tenderloin Sandwiches

Grilled Beef Tenderloin Sandwiches

Ruth Lee, Troy, Ontario

Sweet-sour onions and mushrooms are perfect over this recipe's tender beef and lip-smacking garlic mayonnaise.

✓ *Uses less fat, sugar or salt. Includes Nutrition Facts and Diabetic Exchanges.*

- 1 tablespoon brown sugar
- 2 garlic cloves, minced
- 1/2 teaspoon coarsely ground pepper
- 1/4 teaspoon salt
- 1 beef tenderloin (1 pound)
- 1 whole garlic bulb
- 1/2 teaspoon canola oil
- 1/4 cup *each* fat-free mayonnaise and plain yogurt

ONION TOPPING

- 1 tablespoon olive oil
- 1 large sweet onion, thinly sliced
- 1/2 pound sliced fresh mushrooms
- 2 tablespoons balsamic vinegar
- 1-1/2 teaspoons sugar
- 1/8 teaspoon salt
- 1/8 teaspoon pepper
- 4 slices French bread (3/4 inch thick)
- 1 cup fresh arugula

Combine the first four ingredients; rub over meat. Refrigerate for 2 hours. Remove papery outer skin from garlic (do not peel or separate cloves). Cut top off of garlic. Brush with canola oil. Wrap bulb in heavy-duty foil. Bake at 425° for 30-35 minutes or until softened. Cool for 10-15 minutes. Squeeze garlic into food processor; add mayonnaise and yogurt. Process until smooth; chill.

In a large nonstick skillet, heat olive oil and saute onion for 5 minutes. Reduce heat; cook and stir for 10-12 minutes or until onion is golden. Add mushrooms; cook and stir until tender. Add next four ingredients; cook until reduced slightly.

Coat grill rack with nonstick cooking spray before starting the grill. Grill beef, covered, over medium heat for 5-6 minutes on each side or until meat reaches desired doneness. Let stand for 10 minutes before cutting into 4 slices.

Serve warm on bread with garlic mayonnaise, arugula and onion mixture. **Yield:** 4 servings.

Nutrition Facts: 1 sandwich equals 418 calories, 15 g fat (4 g saturated fat), 75 mg cholesterol, 702 mg sodium, 40 g carbohydrate, 3 g fiber, 31 g protein. **Diabetic Exchanges:** 3 lean meat, 2 starch, 1 vegetable, 1 fat.

Stuffed Barbecue Burgers

Loretta Moe, Grafton, North Dakota

These big burgers are almost a meal by themselves. With a delectable cheese and vegetable filling, they'll surely satisfy any crowd.

- 2 pounds ground beef
- 1 cup (4 ounces) shredded cheese of your choice
- 1/3 cup finely chopped green pepper
- 1/3 cup finely chopped tomato
- 3 fresh mushrooms, finely chopped
- 2 green onions, finely chopped
- 1/2 cup barbecue sauce
- 1 tablespoon sugar
- 4 hamburger buns, split

Shape beef into eight patties. In a large bowl, combine the cheese, green pepper, tomato, mushrooms and onions. Top half of the patties with vegetable mixture. Cover with remaining patties and firmly press edges to seal.

Grill, covered, over medium heat or broil 4 in. from the heat for 3 minutes on each side or until no longer pink. Brush with barbecue sauce and sprinkle with sugar. Grill, covered, or broil 5-6 minutes longer on each side or until no longer pink, basting occasionally. Serve on buns. **Yield:** 4 servings.

Stuffed Barbecue Burgers

Grilled Citrus Steak

Luau Beef Tenderloin Steaks

Lorraine Darocha, Mountain City, Tennessee

Pineapple juice, soy sauce and cider vinegar give these juicy steaks their tangy taste. We found that the sweet and tropical marinade is also good on pork.

✓ *Uses less fat, sugar or salt. Includes Nutrition Facts and Diabetic Exchanges.*

- **1/4 cup unsweetened pineapple juice**
- **1/4 cup reduced-sodium soy sauce**
- **1/4 cup olive oil**
- **2 tablespoons lemon juice**
- **2 tablespoons cider vinegar**
- **6 garlic cloves, minced**
- **1 tablespoon chopped sweet onion**
- **1-1/2 teaspoons ground mustard**
- **1/2 teaspoon minced fresh parsley**
- **4 beef tenderloin steaks (4 ounces each)**

In a small bowl, combine the first nine ingredients. Pour 3/4 cup marinade into a large resealable plastic bag; add the steaks. Seal bag and turn to coat; refrigerate for several hours or overnight. Cover and refrigerate remaining marinade.

Drain steaks and discard marinade. Coat grill rack with nonstick cooking spray before starting the grill. Grill steaks, covered, over medium heat for 6-8 minutes on each side or until meat reaches desired doneness (for medium-rare, a meat thermometer should read 145°; medium, 160°; well-done, 170°). Baste with reserved marinade during the last 2 minutes of cooking. **Yield:** 4 servings.

Nutrition Facts: 1 steak equals 249 calories, 15 g fat (4 g saturated fat), 71 mg cholesterol, 356 mg sodium, 3 g carbohydrate, trace fiber, 25 g protein. **Diabetic Exchanges:** 3 lean meat, 2 fat.

Luau Beef Tenderloin Steaks

Grilled Citrus Steak

Joan Whyte-Elliott, Fenelon Falls, Ontario

We invite someone for dinner almost every weekend, and this recipe has never failed us. It can be prepared in just a few minutes. I like to serve it with vegetables and a salad.

✓ *Uses less fat, sugar or salt. Includes Nutrition Facts and Diabetic Exchanges.*

- **2/3 cup reduced-sugar orange marmalade**
- **1/3 cup reduced-sodium soy sauce**
- **1/3 cup lemon juice**
- **1 tablespoon canola oil**
- **2 pounds boneless beef top round steak (2 inches thick)**

In a large bowl, combine the orange marmalade, soy sauce, lemon juice and oil. Pour 1 cup marinade into a large resealable plastic bag. Score the surface of the steak with shallow diagonal cuts, making diamond shapes. Add the steak to the marinade. Seal bag and turn to coat; refrigerate for 6-8 hours, turning occasionally. Cover and refrigerate remaining marinade.

Coat grill rack with nonstick cooking spray before starting the grill for indirect heat. Drain and discard marinade from beef. Grill beef, covered, over direct medium-hot heat for 6-8 minutes or until browned, turning once. Place beef over indirect heat and continue grilling for 25-30 minutes or until beef reaches desired doneness (for medium-rare, a meat thermometer should read 145°; medium, 160°; well-done, 170°). Baste occasionally with reserved marinade. **Yield:** 6 servings.

Nutrition Facts: 1 serving (4 ounces cooked beef) equals 243 calories, 7 g fat (2 g saturated fat), 96 mg cholesterol, 337 mg sodium, 6 g carbohydrate, 0.55 g fiber, 37 g protein. **Diabetic Exchanges:** 4 lean meat, 1/2 fruit.

Grilled T-Bone Steaks

Steak and Shrimp Kabobs

Karen Mergener, St. Croix, Minnesota

You'll make any get-together special with these attractive kabobs. Cubes of marinated steak are skewered with shrimp, mushrooms, tomatoes, green peppers and onions, then grilled. For picnics, I assemble the kabobs at home and carry them in a large container.

- 1 **cup teriyaki sauce**
- 1 **can (6 ounces) pineapple juice**
- 1/2 **cup packed brown sugar**
- 6 **garlic cloves, minced**
- 1/4 **teaspoon Worcestershire sauce**
- 1/8 **teaspoon pepper**
- 1 **pound boneless beef sirloin steak, cut into 1-inch cubes**
- 1 **pound uncooked large shrimp, peeled and deveined**
- 1 **pound whole fresh mushrooms**
- 2 **large green peppers, cut into 1-inch pieces**
- 2 **medium onions, halved and quartered**
- 1 **pint cherry tomatoes**
- 1-1/2 **teaspoons cornstarch**

In a large bowl, combine the first six ingredients; mix well. Pour half of the marinade into a large resealable plastic bag; add beef. Seal bag and turn to coat; refrigerate for 8 hours or overnight, turning occasionally. Cover and refrigerate remaining marinade.

Drain and discard marinade from beef. On metal or soaked wooden skewers, alternately thread beef, shrimp, mushrooms, green peppers, onions and tomatoes; set aside. In a small saucepan, combine cornstarch and reserved marinade until smooth. Bring to a boil; cook and stir for 1-2 minutes or until sauce is thickened.

Grill kabobs, covered, over indirect medium heat for 6 minutes, turning once. Baste with sauce. Continue turning and basting for 8-10 minutes or until shrimp turn pink and beef reaches desired doneness. **Yield:** 6-8 servings.

Grilled T-Bone Steaks

Beth Wenger, Dayton, Virginia

Grilling brings out the robust flavor of this steak marinade. You can enjoy this recipe while camping or at home.

- 1/2 **cup water**
- 1/2 **cup soy sauce**
- 2 **tablespoons brown sugar**
- 2 **tablespoons lemon juice**
- 2 **tablespoons red wine vinegar**
- 2 **tablespoons vegetable oil**
- 1 **tablespoon Montreal steak seasoning**
- 1/2 **teaspoon garlic powder**
- 1/2 **teaspoon hot pepper sauce**
- 1/4 **teaspoon pepper**
- 4 **beef T-bone steaks (1-inch thick and 3/4 pound *each*)**

In a large resealable plastic bag, combine the first 10 ingredients. Add steaks; seal bag and turn to coat. Refrigerate overnight.

Drain and discard marinade. Grill steaks, covered, over medium heat for 8-12 minutes on each side or until meat reaches desired doneness (for medium-rare, a meat thermometer should read 145°; medium, 160°; well-done, 170°). **Yield:** 4 servings.

Barbecued Chuck Roast

Ardis Gautier, Lamont, Oklahoma

Whether I serve this roast for church dinners, company or family, it is always a hit. To go along with it, my family likes scalloped potatoes, tossed salad and pie. Leftovers make great sandwiches.

- 1/3 **cup cider vinegar**
- 1/4 **cup ketchup**
- 2 **tablespoons vegetable oil**
- 2 **tablespoons soy sauce**
- 1 **tablespoon Worcestershire sauce**
- 1 **teaspoon garlic powder**
- 1 **teaspoon prepared mustard**
- 1 **teaspoon salt**
- 1/4 **teaspoon pepper**
- 1 **boneless chuck roast (2-1/2 to 3 pounds)**
- 1/2 **cup applesauce**

In a large resealable plastic bag or shallow glass container, combine the first nine ingredients; mix well. Add roast and turn to coat. Seal bag or cover container; refrigerate for at least 3 hours, turning occasionally.

Remove roast. Pour marinade into a small saucepan; bring to a boil. Reduce heat; simmer for 15 minutes. Meanwhile, grill roast, covered, over indirect heat for 20 minutes, turning occasionally.

Add applesauce to marinade; brush over roast. Continue basting and turning the roast several times for 1 to 1-1/2 hours or until meat reaches desired doneness (for medium-rare, a meat thermometer should read 145°; medium, 160°; well-done, 170°). **Yield:** 6-8 servings.

Barbecued Chuck Roast

Asian-Style Hamburgers

Peppered T-Bone Steaks

Diane Halferty, Corpus Christi, Texas

When I make these juicy steaks, I brush thin slices of potato with olive oil and grill them alongside the meat. I round out the meal with a spinach and red onion salad on the side and cheesecake for dessert.

> 3 tablespoons steak sauce
> 4-1/2 teaspoons minced fresh thyme *or* 1 teaspoon dried thyme
> 1/4 teaspoon coarsely ground pepper
> 1/4 teaspoon cayenne pepper
> 2 beef T-bone steaks (1 inch thick and 3/4 pound *each*)
> 1/2 teaspoon salt

Coat grill rack with nonstick cooking spray before starting the grill. In a small bowl, combine the steak sauce, thyme, pepper and cayenne. Sprinkle steaks on both sides with salt. Spoon about 2 teaspoons steak sauce mixture on one side of steaks.

Place on grill sauce side down. Grill, covered, over medium heat for 6 minutes. Brush with remaining sauce and turn. Grill 4-6 minutes longer or until meat reaches desired doneness (for medium-rare, a meat thermometer should read 145°; medium, 160°; well-done 170°). **Yield:** 2 servings.

Asian-Style Hamburgers

Myra Innes, Auburn, Kansas

For a change of pace, this marinade gives hamburgers a unique, Asian-inspired flavor.

> 1-1/2 pounds ground beef
> 1/4 cup vegetable oil
> 1/4 cup soy sauce
> 2 tablespoons ketchup
> 1 tablespoon white vinegar
> 2 garlic cloves, minced
> 1/4 teaspoon pepper
> 6 hamburger buns, split

Leaf lettuce and tomato slices, optional

Shape meat into six patties; place in a shallow dish.

In a bowl, whisk together the oil, soy sauce, ketchup, vinegar, garlic and pepper. Set aside 1/4 cup for basting; cover and refrigerate. Pour remaining marinade over the patties. Cover and refrigerate for at least 3 hours.

Grill burgers, uncovered, over medium heat for 5-6 minutes on each side until meat juices run clear, basting occasionally with reserved marinade. Serve on hamburger buns with lettuce leaves and tomato slices if desired. **Yield:** 6 servings.

Quick Tip

When grilling a recipe for two, try to throw a few hamburgers or chicken breasts over the coals as well. The extra meat can be refrigerated for a no-fuss meal the following night.

Peppered T-Bone Steaks

Shape beef into eight thin patties. Top four patties with cheese, onion and jalapenos. Top with remaining patties; press edges firmly to seal. Grill, covered, over medium-hot heat for 8-9 minutes on each side or until no longer pink. Serve on buns. **Yield:** 4 servings.

Editor's Note: When cutting or seeding hot peppers, use rubber or plastic gloves to protect your hands. Avoid touching your face.

Campfire Potatoes

Michelle Isenhoff, Wayland, Michigan

Perfect with beef, chicken and even fish, this flame-broiled side dish can't be beat for taste or convenience.

> 5 medium potatoes, peeled and sliced
> 1/4 cup grated Parmesan cheese
> 2 teaspoons minced fresh parsley
> 3/4 teaspoon garlic powder
> 1/2 teaspoon salt
> 1/8 teaspoon pepper
> 1/4 cup butter, cubed

Place half of the potatoes on a large piece of heavy-duty foil. Sprinkle with Parmesan cheese, parsley, garlic powder, salt and pepper; dot with butter. Top with the remaining potatoes. Fold foil over and seal tightly. Grill, covered, over medium heat for 30-35 minutes or until the potatoes are tender. **Yield:** 4 servings.

Grilled Rib Eye Steaks

Grilled Rib Eye Steaks

Tim Hanchon, Muncie, Indiana

In summer, I love to marinate these steaks overnight, then grill them for family and friends for dinner.

> 1/2 cup soy sauce
> 1/2 cup sliced green onions
> 1/4 cup packed brown sugar
> 2 garlic cloves, minced
> 1/4 teaspoon ground ginger
> 1/4 teaspoon pepper
> 2-1/2 pounds beef rib eye steaks

In a large resealable plastic bag, combine the soy sauce, onions, brown sugar, garlic, ginger and pepper. Add the steaks. Seal bag and turn to coat; refrigerate for 8 hours or overnight.

Drain and discard marinade. Grill steaks, uncovered, over medium-hot heat for 8-10 minutes or until the meat reaches desired doneness (for medium-rare, a meat thermometer should read 145°; medium, 160°; well-done, 170°). **Yield:** 2-4 servings and about 1-1/4 pounds leftover steak.

Jalapeno Swiss Burgers

Jeanine Richardson, Floresville, Texas

Mexican culture greatly influences our cuisine, and we eat a lot of spicy foods. In this recipe, the mellow flavor of Swiss cheese cuts the heat of the jalapenos.

> 2 pounds ground beef
> 4 slices Swiss cheese
> 1 small onion, thinly sliced
> 2 to 3 pickled jalapeno peppers, seeded and julienned
> 4 hamburger buns, split

Jalapeno Swiss Burgers

No-Fuss Sweet Potatoes

Lillian Neer, Long Eddy, New York

I love trying new recipes, so when my son-in-law suggested we grill sweet potatoes, I said yes. Served with steak, they're a great change of pace from traditional baked potatoes...and they're pretty, too.

> 2 large sweet potatoes, halved
> lengthwise
> 2 tablespoons butter, softened
> Garlic salt and pepper to taste
> 2 teaspoons honey

Cut two pieces of heavy-duty foil (about 18 in. x 12 in.); place a potato half on each. Spread cut side with butter. Sprinkle with garlic salt and pepper. Top each potato with another half. Fold foil over potatoes and seal tightly. Grill, covered, over medium-hot heat for 30 minutes or until tender, turning once. To serve, fluff potatoes with a fork and drizzle with honey. **Yield:** 4 servings.

Steaks with Cucumber Sause

Red Potato Skewers

Dawn Finch, Prosser, Washington

A seasoned mayonnaise mixture keeps these quartered red potatoes moist and heavenly. My mouth waters just thinking about how they'll taste hot off the grill.

> 2 pounds red potatoes (about 6
> medium), quartered
> 1/2 cup water
> 1/2 cup mayonnaise
> 1/4 cup chicken broth
> 2 teaspoons dried oregano
> 1/2 teaspoon garlic salt
> 1/2 teaspoon onion powder

Place the potatoes and water in an ungreased microwave-safe 2-qt. dish. Cover and microwave on high for 10-12 minutes or until almost tender, stirring once; drain. In a large bowl, combine the remaining ingredients; add potatoes. Cover and refrigerate for 1 hour.

Drain, reserving mayonnaise mixture. Thread the potatoes onto metal or soaked wooden skewers. Grill, uncovered, over medium heat for 4 minutes. Turn; brush with reserved mayonnaise mixture. Grill 4 minutes longer or until potatoes are tender and golden brown. **Yield:** 6 servings.

Editor's Note: This recipe was tested in a 1,100-watt microwave.

No-Fuss Sweet Potatoes

Steaks with Cucumber Sauce

Erika Aylward, Clinton, Michigan

Tender steaks, marinated with teriyaki sauce, are accompanied by a creamy cucumber sauce in this hearty dish.

> 4 boneless beef New York strip
> steaks (8 to 10 ounces *each*)
> 3/4 cup teriyaki sauce
> 1/2 cup chopped seeded peeled
> cucumber
> 1/2 cup sour cream
> 1/2 cup mayonnaise
> 1 tablespoon minced chives
> 1/2 to 1 teaspoon dill weed
> 1/4 teaspoon salt

Place steaks in a large resealable plastic bag; add teriyaki sauce. Seal bag and turn to coat; refrigerate overnight. In a bowl, combine the cucumber, sour cream, mayonnaise, chives, dill and salt. Cover and refrigerate.

Drain and discard marinade. Grill steaks, uncovered, over medium-hot heat for 4-5 minutes on each side or until meat reaches desired doneness (for medium-rare, a meat thermometer should read 145°; medium, 160°; well-done, 170°). Serve with cucumber sauce. **Yield:** 4 servings.

Meat Loaf Hamburgers

Sandra Pichon, Slidell, Louisiana

These tender, mellow-tasting burgers will please everyone. They're a nice alternative to plain ground beef patties and are very popular whenever I serve them.

1-1/2	pounds ground beef
1	cup (8 ounces) sour cream
1-1/4	cups crushed cornflakes
1	tablespoon diced onion
1/2 to 1	teaspoon salt
1/8	teaspoon pepper
8	kaiser *or* hamburger buns, split

Lettuce leaves

Tomato slices

In a large bowl, gently mix the first six ingredients; shape into eight patties. Grill, broil or pan-fry until the meat is no longer pink. Serve on buns with lettuce and tomato. **Yield:** 8 servings.

Caesar New York Strips

Melissa Morton, Philadelphia, Pennsylvania

I season New York strip steaks with a Caesar dressing mixture, then grill them for a tasty entree that's ready in minutes. As a side dish, I like to serve baked potatoes topped with chunky salsa and sour cream.

4	tablespoons Caesar salad dressing, *divided*
2	teaspoons garlic powder
1	teaspoon salt
1	teaspoon coarsely ground pepper
2	New York strip steaks (12 ounces *each*)

In a small bowl, combine 2 tablespoons salad dressing, garlic powder, salt and pepper. Spoon over both sides of the steaks.

Grill, covered, over medium heat or broil 4 in. from the heat for 7-9 minutes on each side or until meat reaches desired doneness (for medium-rare, a meat thermometer should read 145°; medium, 160°; well-done, 170°), basting occasionally with remaining salad dressing. Cut steaks in half to serve. **Yield:** 4 servings.

Meat Loaf Hamburgers

Potato Pockets

Denise Nebel, Wayland, Iowa

Our sons like to help me assemble potatoes, carrots and onions into foil packages that we can put on the grill. The sprinkling of cheese adds a nice touch.

4	medium potatoes, julienned
3	carrots, julienned
1/3	cup chopped red onion
2	tablespoons butter
1/2	teaspoon salt, optional
1/8	teaspoon pepper
1/2	cup shredded Parmesan *or* cheddar cheese

Divide the potatoes, carrots and onion equally between four pieces of heavy-duty aluminum foil (about 18 in. x 12 in.). Top with butter; sprinkle with salt if desired and pepper. Bring opposite short ends of foil together over vegetables and fold down several times. Fold unsealed ends toward vegetables and crimp tightly.

Grill, covered, over medium heat for 10-15 minutes on each side or until potatoes are tender. Remove from grill. Open foil and sprinkle with cheese; reseal. Let stand for 5 minutes or until the cheese melts. **Yield:** 4 servings.

Ceasar New York Strips

Country-Style Pot Roast (p.

Meat & Potato Lover's Cookbook

Chapter 5

Classic Roasts

Whether you want to prepare a show-stopping holiday dinner or make Sunday's meal extra-special, the end result will be tender and delicious with any of these time-honored roast recipes.

Italian Pot Roast

Favorite Roast

Leona Therou, Overland Park, Kansas

I love cooking a pot roast on the weekend because it can simmer for hours while I'm doing other things. This hearty beef roast with potatoes and carrots makes enough for a family of four with plenty left over.

- 1 **boneless beef rump roast (4 pounds)**
- 2 **tablespoons vegetable oil**
- 2 **teaspoons salt**
- 1/2 **teaspoon pepper**
- 1/2 **teaspoon dried thyme**
- 1 **bay leaf**
- 3 **cups water,** *divided*
- 8 **medium potatoes, peeled and quartered**
- 8 **large carrots, cut into 2-inch chunks**
- 1 **pound small onions, peeled**
- 1/2 **cup all-purpose flour**
- 1/2 **teaspoon browning sauce, optional**

Additional salt and pepper to taste

In a Dutch oven, brown the roast in oil. Combine the salt, pepper and thyme; sprinkle over meat. Add bay leaf and 2 cups water; bring to a boil. Reduce heat; cover and simmer for 2-1/2 hours.

Add the potatoes, carrots and onions. Cover and simmer 45 minutes longer or until meat and vegetables are tender. Remove roast and vegetables to a serving platter; keep warm. Discard bay leaf.

Skim fat from pan juices; add enough water to pan juices to measure 2 cups. In a bowl, combine flour and remaining water until smooth; stir into juices. Bring to a boil; cook and stir for 2 minutes or until thickened and bubbly. Stir in browning sauce if desired. Season with salt and pepper. Slice roast; serve with vegetables and gravy. **Yield:** 8 servings.

Italian Pot Roast

Georgie Seidler, Pine Grove, California

I fix this pot roast when my grown children come over. I know it's one of their favorites, because all of them have asked for the recipe.

- 1 **beef rump roast (4 to 5 pounds)**
- 1 **to 2 teaspoons salt**
- 2 **tablespoons vegetable oil**
- 2 **garlic cloves, minced**
- 1/2 **teaspoon dried parsley flakes**
- 1/2 **teaspoon pepper**
- 2 **carrots, sliced**
- 1 **whole onion, studded with 2 whole cloves**
- 1 **can (15 ounces) tomato puree**
- 1/2 **cup water** *or* **red wine**
- 1/2 **teaspoon beef bouillon granules**

Cooked egg noodles

Rub roast with salt. In a Dutch oven, brown roast in oil. Add all remaining ingredients except noodles. Bring to a boil; reduce heat and simmer, covered, about 2-3 hours or until meat is tender.

Discard onion. Remove roast; cut into slices. Serve over noodles with gravy. **Yield:** 8-10 servings.

Favorite Roast

Oriental Pot Roast

Donna Staley, Randleman, North Carolina

I love Oriental food, so this pot roast satisfies my cravings. The original recipe called for spinach, but I use sugar snap peas and carrots instead. Sometimes I serve the roast, vegetables and pineapple over rice or egg noodles.

- 1 **boneless beef rump roast (3 pounds)**
- 1 **tablespoon vegetable oil**
- 1 **large onion, chopped**
- 1 **can (20 ounces) pineapple chunks**
- 3 **tablespoons soy sauce**
- 1 **garlic cloves, minced**
- 1 **teaspoon ground ginger**
- 3 **celery ribs, sliced**
- 2 **medium carrots, sliced**
- 1 **cup fresh sugar snap peas**
- 1 **cup sliced fresh mushrooms**
- 1 **to 2 tablespoons cornstarch**
- 1/4 **cup cold water**

In a Dutch oven over medium heat, brown roast in oil on all sides; drain. Add onion. Drain pineapple, reserving juice; set pineapple aside. In a small bowl, combine the pineapple juice, soy sauce, garlic and ginger. Pour over roast. Bring to a boil. Reduce heat; cover and simmer for 2 hours or until meat is almost tender.

Add the celery and carrots. Cover and simmer for 20 minutes or until vegetables are crisp-tender. Add the peas, mushrooms and reserved pineapple. Cover and simmer 15 minutes longer or until the vegetables and the meat are tender.

Remove the roast, vegetables and pineapple; keep warm. Skim fat from pan drippings. Combine cornstarch and cold water until smooth; gradually stir into the drippings.

Bring to a boil; cook and stir for 2 minutes or until thickened.

Slice roast across the grain. Serve meat, vegetables and pineapple with gravy. **Yield:** 6 servings.

Oriental Pot Roast

Savory Beef Dinner

Lee Leuschner, Calgary, Alberta

This old-fashioned pot roast with smooth pan gravy evokes memories of dinners at Mom's or Grandma's. My husband and I used to raise cattle, so I prepared a lot of beef—and we think this is the best.

- 1 **rolled boneless beef chuck roast (6 pounds)**
- 2 **tablespoons vegetable oil**

Salt and coarsely ground pepper

- 1 **large onion, coarsely chopped**
- 2 **medium carrots, coarsely chopped**
- 1 **celery rib, coarsely chopped**
- 2 **cups water**
- 1 **can (14-1/2 ounces) beef broth**
- 2 **bay leaves**

GRAVY

- 1/4 **cup butter, cubed**
- 1/4 **cup all-purpose flour**
- 1 **teaspoon lemon juice**
- 4 **to 5 drops hot pepper sauce**

In a large skillet over medium-high heat, brown roast in oil on all sides. Transfer to a large roasting pan; season with salt and pepper. Add the onion, carrots and celery.

In a large saucepan, bring the water, broth and bay leaves to a boil. Pour over roast and vegetables. Cover and bake at 350° for 2-1/2 to 3 hours or until meat is tender, turning once.

Remove roast to a serving platter and keep warm. For gravy, strain pan juices, reserving 2 cups. Discard vegetables and bay leaves. In a large saucepan over medium heat, melt butter; stir in flour until smooth. Gradually stir in pan juices. Bring to a boil; cook and stir for 2 minutes or until thickened. Stir in lemon juice and hot pepper sauce. Serve with roast. **Yield:** 14-16 servings.

Editor's Note: Ask your butcher to tie two 3-pound chuck roasts together to form a rolled chuck roast.

Savory Beef Dinner

Braised Beef With Barley

June Formanek, Belle Plaine, Iowa

Braising works well for less tender cuts of meat, and brings out the flavor of the chuck roast in this recipe. Barley, mushrooms and peas are a wonderful addition to the meal.

- 1 **boneless chuck roast (2 to 2-1/2 pounds)**
- 1 **tablespoon vegetable oil**
- 1 **medium onion, chopped**
- 1/2 **pound fresh mushrooms, sliced**
- 3 **garlic cloves, minced**
- 1 **can (14-1/2 ounces) beef broth**
- 1 **bay leaf**
- 1-1/2 **teaspoons salt**
- 1/4 **teaspoon pepper**
- 1/2 **cup medium pearl barley**
- 1 **cup frozen peas**
- 1/3 **cup sour cream, optional**

In a Dutch oven, brown meat in oil on all sides over medium-high heat. Remove roast and set aside. Drain, reserving 1 tablespoon of drippings.

Saute the onion, mushrooms and garlic in drippings until tender. Return roast to the pan. Add the broth, bay leaf, salt and pepper; bring to a boil. Reduce heat; cover and simmer for 1-1/2 hours. Add barley. Cover and simmer for 45 minutes or until meat and barley are tender. Add peas; cover and simmer for 5 minutes or until peas are tender. Discard bay leaf.

Set the roast and barley aside; keep warm. Skim fat from pan juices. If desired, add sour cream to the pan juices; stir until heated through over low heat (do not boil). Slice roast; serve with barley and gravy. **Yield:** 6 servings.

Bavarian Pot Roast

Bavarian Pot Roast

Patricia Gasmund, Rockford, Illinois

I grew up eating pot roast but disliked it until I got this recipe at a church social and changed a few ingredients. My 7-year-old especially enjoys the seasoned apple gravy.

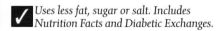 *Uses less fat, sugar or salt. Includes Nutrition Facts and Diabetic Exchanges.*

- 1 **boneless beef top round roast (about 4 pounds), halved**
- 1-1/2 **cups apple juice**
- 1 **can (8 ounces) tomato sauce**
- 1 **small onion, chopped**
- 2 **tablespoons white vinegar**
- 1 **tablespoon salt**
- 2 to 3 **teaspoons ground cinnamon**
- 1 **tablespoon minced fresh gingerroot**
- 1/4 **cup cornstarch**
- 1/2 **cup water**

In a Dutch oven coated with nonstick cooking spray, brown roast on all sides over medium-high heat; drain. Transfer to a 5-qt. slow cooker. In a bowl, combine the juice, tomato sauce, onion, vinegar, salt, cinnamon and ginger; pour over roast. Cover and cook on high for 5-7 hours.

In a small bowl, combine cornstarch and water until smooth; stir into cooking juices until well combined. Cover and cook 1 hour longer or until the meat is tender and gravy begins to thicken. **Yield:** 12 servings.

Nutrition Facts: 1 serving (4 ounces cooked beef with 1/2 cup gravy) equals 230 calories, 7 g fat (2 g saturated fat), 96 mg cholesterol, 753 mg sodium, 8 g carbohydrate, 1 g fiber, 32 g protein. **Diabetic Exchanges:** 4 lean meat, 1/2 fruit.

Quick Tip

Roasts are usually best reheated in the oven. Slice the meat and cover it with some of the pan juices. Cover the baking dish and heat through.

Apple and Onion Beef Roast

Rachel Koistinen, Hayti, South Dakota

Rely on your slow cooker to help prepare this moist pot roast. I thicken the juices to make a pleasing apple gravy that's wonderful over the beef slices and onions.

- 1 **boneless beef sirloin tip roast (3 pounds), cut in half**
- 1 **cup water**
- 1 **teaspoon seasoned salt**
- 1/2 **teaspoon reduced-sodium soy sauce**
- 1/2 **teaspoon Worcestershire sauce**
- 1/4 **teaspoon garlic powder**
- 1 **large tart apple, quartered**
- 1 **large onion, sliced**
- 2 **tablespoons cornstarch**
- 2 **tablespoons cold water**
- 1/8 **teaspoon browning sauce**

In a large nonstick skillet coated with nonstick cooking spray, brown roast on all sides. Transfer to a 5-qt. slow cooker. Add water to the skillet, stirring to loosen any browned bits; pour over roast. Sprinkle with seasoned salt, soy sauce, Worcestershire sauce and garlic powder. Top with apple and onion. Cover and cook on low for 5-6 hours or until the meat is tender.

Remove roast and onion; let stand for 15 minutes before slicing. Strain cooking liquid into a saucepan, discarding apple. Bring liquid to a boil; cook until reduced to 2 cups, about 15 minutes. Combine cornstarch and cold water until smooth; stir in browning sauce. Stir into cooking liquid. Bring to a boil; cook and stir for 2 minutes or until thickened. Serve over beef and onion. **Yield:** 8 servings.

Garlic Chunk Roast

Apple and Onion Beef Roast

Garlic Chuck Roast

Janet Boyer, Nemacolin, Pennsylvania

Having never made a roast before, I experimented with a few ingredients to come up with this hearty, all-in-one meal. Not only is it easy, but the tender entree gets terrific flavor from garlic, onion and bay leaves.

- 1 **boneless beef chuck roast (3 pounds)**
- 15 **garlic cloves, peeled**
- 1 **teaspoon salt**
- 1/4 **teaspoon pepper**
- 2 **tablespoons vegetable oil**
- 5 **bay leaves**
- 1 **large onion, thinly sliced**
- 2 **tablespoons butter, melted**
- 1-1/2 **cups water**
- 1 **pound baby carrots**

With a sharp knife, cut 15 slits in roast; insert garlic into slits. Sprinkle meat with salt and pepper. In a Dutch oven, brown meat in oil; drain. Place bay leaves on top of roast; top with onion slices. Drizzle with butter. Add water to pan. Cover and bake at 325° for 1-1/2 hours.

Baste roast with pan juices; add carrots. Cover and bake 45-60 minutes longer or until meat and carrots are tender. Discard bay leaves. Let roast stand for 10 minutes before slicing. Thicken pan juices if desired. **Yield:** 6-8 servings.

Slow-Cooked Coffee Pot Roast

Janet Dominick, Bagley, Minnesota

Slow cooked to tender perfection, this roast features a savory coffee marinade.

- 2 **medium onions, thinly sliced**
- 2 **garlic cloves, minced**
- 1 **boneless beef chuck roast (3-1/2 to 4 pounds), quartered**
- 1 **cup brewed coffee**
- 1/4 **cup soy sauce**
- 1/4 **cup cornstarch**
- 6 **tablespoons cold water**

Place half of the onions in a 5-qt. slow cooker. Top with garlic and half of the beef. Top with remaining onion and beef. Combine coffee and soy sauce; pour over beef. Cover and cook on low for 9-10 hours or until meat is tender.

Combine cornstarch and water until smooth; stir into cooking juices. Cover and cook on high for 30 minutes or until gravy is thickened. **Yield:** 10-12 servings.

Quick Tip

Beat the temptation to peek when preparing a roast in your slow cooker! As much as 40% of the heat can be lost from a slow cooker when the lid is lifted...even for a moment.

Marinated Chuck Roast

Mary Lee Baker, Enon, Ohio

It's the simple marinade of orange juice, soy sauce, brown sugar and Worcestershire sauce that makes this beef roast so tasty and tender.

1/2 cup orange juice
3 tablespoons soy sauce
3 tablespoons brown sugar
1 teaspoon Worcestershire sauce
1 boneless beef chuck roast (3 to 4 pounds)

In a large resealable plastic bag, combine the orange juice, soy sauce, brown sugar and Worcestershire sauce; add the roast. Seal bag and turn to coat; refrigerate for 8 hours or overnight.

Pour the marinade into a Dutch oven. Bring to a boil; boil for 2 minutes. Add roast to the pan. Cover and bake at 325° for 3 to 3-1/2 hours or until the meat is tender.

Let stand for 10 minutes before slicing. Thicken juices for gravy if desired. **Yield:** 8-10 servings.

Marinated Chuck Roast

Smoky Beef Roast

Myra Innes, Auburn, Kansas

When the weather isn't ideal for grilling, but you long for that barbecue flavor, try this delicious recipe. You get the outdoor flavor indoors with this juicy roast.

1/4 cup water
1 tablespoon Liquid Smoke, optional
1 tablespoon brown sugar
1 teaspoon celery salt
1 teaspoon onion salt
1/2 teaspoon ground nutmeg
1/2 teaspoon mustard seed
1/4 teaspoon pepper
1 boneless beef chuck roast (2 to 3 pounds)
1/4 cup barbecue sauce

In a large resealable plastic bag or shallow container, combine the first eight ingredients. Add roast. Seal bag or cover container; refrigerate for 8 hours, turning once.

Drain and discard marinade. Place roast in a greased 2-1/2-qt. baking pan. Cover and bake at 325° for 1-1/2 to 2 hours. Baste with barbecue sauce. Bake, uncovered, 10-12 minutes longer or until beef is fork-tender. **Yield:** 4-6 servings.

Home-Style Roast Beef

Home-Style Roast Beef

Sandra Furman-Krajewski Amsterdam, New York

A very moist roast, this gains richness from the gravy, and the bacon gives it a somewhat different taste. For variety, you can cube the roast and serve it over rice with gravy...or cube and mix it with noodles, gravy and vegetables if you'd like to make it into a casserole.

1 beef bottom round roast (10 to 12 pounds)
1 can (14-1/2 ounces) chicken broth
1 can (10-1/4 ounces) beef gravy
1 can (10-3/4 ounces) condensed cream of celery soup, undiluted
1/4 cup water
1/4 cup Worcestershire sauce
1/4 cup soy sauce
3 tablespoons dried parsley flakes
3 tablespoons dill weed
2 tablespoons dried thyme
4-1/2 teaspoons garlic powder
1 teaspoon celery salt
Pepper to taste
1 large onion, sliced 1/4 inch thick
8 bacon strips
1/4 cup butter, cubed

Place roast in a large roasting pan with fat side up. Prick meat in several places with a meat fork. Combine broth, gravy, soup, water, Worcestershire sauce and soy sauce; pour over roast. Sprinkle with seasonings. Arrange onion slices over roast. Place bacon strips diagonally over onion. Dot with butter.

Bake, uncovered, at 325° for 2-1/2 to 3-1/2 hours or until the meat reaches desired doneness (for medium-rare, a meat thermometer should read 145°; medium, 160°; well-done, 170°). Let stand for 15 minutes before slicing. **Yield:** 25-30 servings.

Herbed Beef Rib Roast

Donna Conlin, Gilmour, Ontario

This is one of my favorite ways to prepare a roast because it turns out so tender and flavorful. My husband and our six children just love it, and I'm sure that you and your family will feel the same.

- 1 tablespoon garlic powder
- 1 tablespoon ground mustard
- 1 to 2 teaspoons salt
- 1 to 2 teaspoons pepper
- 1 beef rib roast (6 to 8 pounds)
- 1/4 cup water
- 1/4 cup beef broth
- 1 tablespoon red wine vinegar *or* cider vinegar

Combine the garlic powder, mustard, salt and pepper; rub over entire roast. Place roast fat side up in a shallow roasting pan. Pour water, broth and vinegar into pan.

Bake, uncovered, at 350° for 2-3/4 to 3 hours, basting frequently with pan juices, or until meat reaches desired doneness (for medium-rare, a meat thermometer should read 145°; medium, 160°; well-done, 170°). Let stand for 10-15 minutes before slicing. **Yield:** 10-12 servings.

Holiday Roast

Herbed Beef Rib Roast

Cranberry Pot Roast

Jim Ulberg, Elk Rapids, Michigan

A tangy cranberry sauce smothers this succulent beef roast. Convenient canned whole-berry cranberries make it easy to create the luscious sauce. It's great for autumn.

- 2 tablespoons all-purpose flour
- 1 teaspoon salt
- 1/2 teaspoon pepper
- 1 beef chuck roast (4 to 5 pounds)
- 2 tablespoons shortening
- 1 medium onion
- 6 whole cloves
- 1 cup water
- 1 medium carrot, shredded
- 2 cinnamon sticks (3 inches)
- 1 can (16 ounces) whole-berry cranberry sauce
- 2 tablespoons cider vinegar

Combine flour, salt and pepper; rub over roast. In a Dutch oven, brown roast in shortening. Cut onion in half and stick the cloves into it. Add onion, water, carrot and cinnamon to pan. Bring to a boil. Reduce heat; cover and simmer for 2-1/2 hours.

Add additional water if needed. Spoon off fat. Combine cranberry sauce and vinegar; pour over the roast. Cover and simmer 45 minutes longer or until meat is tender. Discard onion, cloves and cinnamon. **Yield:** 10-12 servings.

Holiday Roast

Carol Jackson, South Berwick, Maine

The pungent mixture of herbs and garlic turns this impressive roast into a real treat. Try it yourself and see. Our children and grandchildren look forward to feasting on it at Christmastime and other special family occasions we share.

- 1 boneless beef rib roast (4 to 5 pounds)
- 2 to 3 garlic cloves, thinly sliced
- 1 teaspoon salt
- 1/2 teaspoon pepper
- 1/2 teaspoon dried basil
- 1/2 teaspoon dried parsley flakes
- 1/2 teaspoon dried marjoram

Cut 15-20 slits in the roast; insert garlic. Combine salt, pepper, basil, parsley and marjoram; rub over roast. Place fat side up on a rack in a roasting pan. Bake, uncovered, at 325° for 2 to 2-1/2 hours or until meat reaches the desired doneness (for medium-rare, a meat thermometer should read 145°; medium, 160°; well-done, 170°). **Yield:** 8-10 servings.

Peppered Rib Roast

Peppered Rib Roast

Mary Welch, Sturgeon Bay, Wisconsin

A co-worker shared this restaurant recipe with me. The marinade tenderizes the meat, and the drippings make a savory sauce to accompany the moist beef slices.

- 1/4 cup coarsely ground pepper
- 1/2 teaspoon ground cardamom
- 1 boneless beef rib eye roast (5 to 6 pounds)
- 1 cup soy sauce
- 3/4 cup red wine vinegar
- 1 tablespoon tomato paste
- 1 teaspoon paprika
- 1/2 teaspoon garlic powder
- 1-1/2 teaspoons cornstarch
- 1/4 cup cold water

Combine the pepper and cardamom; rub over roast. In a gallon-size resealable plastic bag, combine the soy sauce, vinegar, tomato paste, paprika and garlic powder; add the roast. Seal bag and turn to coat; refrigerate overnight.

Drain and discard marinade. Place roast on a rack in a shallow roasting pan. Cover and bake at 350° for 2 to 2-3/4 hours or until meat reaches desired doneness (for medium-rare, a meat thermometer should read 145°; medium, 160°; well-done, 170°). Let stand for 20 minutes before carving.

Meanwhile, for gravy, pour the pan drippings and loosened brown bits into a saucepan; skim fat. Combine cornstarch and cold water until smooth; gradually stir into the drippings. Bring to a boil; cook and stir for 2 minutes or until thickened. Serve with the roast. **Yield:** 16-18 servings.

Caraway Beef Roast

Beverly Swanson, Red Oak, Iowa

It seems there aren't many beef roasts that are both extra-special and extra-easy. This one is, though. There have been many Sundays when I've put it in the oven as we're walking out the door to go to church and had no trouble getting it on the table right around noon.

- 3 tablespoons vegetable oil
- 1 beef rump *or* chuck roast (3 pounds)
- 1 cup hot water
- 1-1/2 teaspoons beef bouillon granules
- 1/4 cup ketchup
- 1 tablespoon Worcestershire sauce
- 1 tablespoon dried minced onion
- 1 teaspoon salt
- 1/2 teaspoon pepper
- 2 teaspoons caraway seeds
- 2 bay leaves
- 2 tablespoons all-purpose flour
- 1/4 cup water

Cooked potatoes and carrots, optional

In a Dutch oven, heat oil over medium-high. Brown roast on all sides. Drain. Combine water, bouillon, ketchup, Worcestershire sauce, onion, salt, pepper and caraway. Pour over roast. Add bay leaves. Cover and bake at 325° for 3 hours or until tender. Remove roast to a warm serving platter.

Combine flour and water. Stir into pan juices. Bring to a boil, stirring constantly. Cook until thickened, adding additional water if necessary. Remove bay leaves. Serve with cooked potatoes and carrots if desired. **Yield:** 12 servings.

Quick Tip

Is your spice rack looking bare? You can season beef or even pork roasts with a little Worcestershire sauce and some chopped onion. Add a bay leaf if you've got one on hand.

Caraway Beef Roast

Nutrition Facts: 1 serving (prepared with low-sodium beef broth; calculated without salt) equals 301 calories, 14 g fat (0 saturated fat), 82 mg cholesterol, 59 mg sodium, 16 g carbohydrate, 0 fiber, 27 g protein. **Diabetic Exchanges:** 3 lean meat, 1 starch, 1 vegetable.

Prime Rib with Horseradish Sauce

Dilled Chuck Roast

Judy Poor, Overland Park, Kansas

This trouble-free pot roast is wonderful family fare and a favorite to serve guests. I serve it with noodles or rice. I owe my love of creative cooking to my late mother who was a professional cook.

- 1 **bone-in beef arm pot roast** *or* **chuck roast (about 3-1/2 pounds)**
- 2 **tablespoons vegetable oil**
- 1 **tablespoon dill seed**
- 1 **teaspoon salt**
- 1/4 **teaspoon pepper**
- 1 **cup water**
- 2 **tablespoons white wine vinegar**
- 3 **tablespoons all-purpose flour**
- 1-1/4 **cups sour cream**
- 2 **teaspoons dill weed**

In a Dutch oven, brown roast in oil on all sides; drain. Sprinkle with dill seed, salt and pepper. Add water and vinegar to the pan. Cover and bake at 325° for 3 hours or until meat is tender.

Remove roast and keep warm. Pour drippings into a measuring cup. Strain and skim fat, reserving 3 tablespoons fat and all of the drippings. In a saucepan, heat reserved fat and drippings; stir in flour until blended. Bring to a boil; cook and stir for 1 minute or until thickened.

Reduce heat to low. Stir in the sour cream and dill weed heat through (do not boil). Serve with the roast. **Yield:** 10-12 servings.

Dilled Chuck Roast

Prime Rib with Horseradish Sauce

Paula Zsiray, Logan, Utah

A menu featuring tender prime rib is festive yet simple to prepare. A pepper rub and a mild horseradish sauce complement the beef's great flavor.

- 1 **semi-boneless beef rib roast (4 to 6 pounds)**
- 1 **tablespoon olive oil**
- 1 **to 2 teaspoons coarsely ground pepper**

HORSERADISH SAUCE
- 1 **cup (8 ounces) sour cream**
- 3 **to 4 tablespoons prepared horseradish**
- 1 **teaspoon coarsely ground pepper**
- 1/8 **teaspoon Worcestershire sauce**

Brush roast with oil; rub with pepper. Place roast, fat side up, in a shallow roasting pan. Bake, uncovered, at 450° for 15 minutes.

Reduce heat to 325°. Bake for 2-3/4 hours or until meat reaches desired doneness (for medium-rare, a meat thermometer should read 145°; medium, 160°; well-done, 170°), basting with pan drippings every 30 minutes. Let stand for 10-15 minutes before slicing. Meanwhile, in a small bowl, combine the sauce ingredients. Serve with beef. **Yield:** 6-8 servings.

Sage Pot Roast

Noami Giddis, Grawn, Michigan

The addition of sage in this pot roast really adds a unique flavor the whole family will love. Or, serve it at your next company dinner. You're sure to get rave reviews!

✓ *Uses less fat, sugar or salt. Includes Nutrition Facts and Diabetic Exchanges.*

- 1 **boneless beef chuck roast (about 5 pounds)**
- 1 **tablespoon vegetable oil**
- 1 **to 2 teaspoons rubbed dried sage**
- 1/2 **teaspoon salt, optional**
- 1/4 **teaspoon pepper**
- 1 **cup beef broth**
- 6 **medium red potatoes (about 2 pounds), cut in half**
- 3 **to 4 carrots, cut into 2-inch pieces**
- 2 **medium onions, quartered**
- 1/4 **cup water**
- 5 **teaspoons cornstarch**

In a Dutch oven, brown roast on both sides in oil. Season with sage, salt if desired, and pepper. Add beef broth. Cover and bake at 325° for 2-1/2 hours.

Add potatoes, carrots and onions. Cover and bake 1 hour longer or until the meat is tender and vegetables are cooked. Remove roast and vegetables to a serving platter and keep warm.

Combine water and cornstarch; stir into pan juices. Cook until thickened and bubbly. Serve with the roast. **Yield:** 12 servings.

Zesty Beef Roast

Joan Enerson, Waupaca, Wisconsin

One day when I ran out of ketchup, I substituted horseradish in the sauce for the meatballs I was making. It was delicious, so next I decided to try it on a roast. It, too, was a winner.

> 1 **boneless beef sirloin tip roast** *or* **boneless beef rump roast (3 pounds)**
> 2 **tablespoons vegetable oil**
> 1 **cup beef broth**
> 1/4 **to 1/3 cup prepared horseradish**
> 1 **cup chopped onion**
> 1/4 **teaspoon salt**
> 1/4 **teaspoon pepper**
> 1/3 **cup all-purpose flour**
> 2/3 **cup cold water**

In a Dutch oven, brown roast on all sides in oil. Add broth. Spread horseradish over roast; sprinkle with onion, salt and pepper. Cover and bake at 350° for 2 hours or until tender, basting frequently. Remove roast from the pan; let stand for 10 minutes.

Meanwhile, pour the pan juices into a large measuring cup; add water to equal 2 cups. Return to pan. Combine flour and cold water until smooth; gradually stir into pan juices. Bring to a boil; cook and stir for 2 minutes. Add additional water if a thinner gravy is desired. Slice roast; serve with gravy. **Yield:** 6-8 servings.

Stuffed Sirloin Roast

Stuffed Sirloin Roast

Jackie Hannahs, Fountain, Michigan

Bacon on top gives this roast a slightly smoky flavor. With a colorful stuffing, slices look lovely on a platter.

> 9 **bacon strips,** *divided*
> 1 **medium onion, chopped**
> 3/4 **cup chopped celery**
> 1 **large carrot, chopped**
> 1/3 **cup dry bread crumbs**
> 2 **teaspoons dried parsley flakes**
> 1/4 **teaspoon garlic powder**
> 1/8 **teaspoon pepper**
> 1 **boneless beef sirloin tip roast (3 to 4 pounds)**

In a large skillet, cook six bacon strips over medium heat until crisp. Remove to paper towels; drain, reserving 3 tablespoons drippings. Crumble bacon and set aside. In the drippings, saute the onion, celery and carrot until crisp-tender. Remove from the heat; stir in the bread crumbs, parsley, garlic powder, pepper and crumbled bacon. Let stand until the liquid is absorbed.

Cut a lengthwise slit down the center of the roast to within 1/2 in. of bottom. Open roast so it lies flat; cover with plastic wrap. Flatten to 1-in. thickness. Remove plastic; spread stuffing over meat to within 1 in. of edges. Close roast and tie at 1-in. intervals with kitchen string.

Place on a rack in a shallow roasting pan. Cut remaining bacon strips in half; arrange over top of roast. Bake, uncovered, at 325° for 1-1/2 to 2 hours or until meat reached desired doneness (for medium-rare, a meat thermometer should read 145°; medium, 160°; well-done, 170°). Let stand for 10 minutes before slicing. **Yield:** 10-14 servings.

Zesty Beef Roast

Chuck Roast with Homemade Noodles

Chuck Roast with Homemade Noodles

Gloria Grant, Sterling, Illinois

The whole family loves Mom's tender beef and hearty noodles. Simmered in beef broth, the noodles taste wonderfully old-fashioned. Mom has to make a huge batch since even the grandchildren gobble them up.

- 1 boneless beef chuck roast (3 to 4 pounds)
- 1/2 cup chopped onion
- 2 tablespoons vegetable oil
- 2-1/2 cups water, *divided*
- 1 cup all-purpose flour
- 1/2 teaspoon salt
- 1 egg
- 2 tablespoons milk
- 1 can (14 ounces) beef broth

Pepper to taste

In a Dutch oven, brown roast and onion in oil. Add 1/2 cup of water. Cover and bake at 325° for 2-1/2 to 3 hours or until the meat is tender.

Meanwhile, for noodles, combine flour and salt in a bowl; make a well in the center. Beat egg and milk; pour into well. Stir to form a stiff dough. Turn onto a well-floured surface; roll into a 15-in. x 12-in. rectangle. Cut into 1/8-in. strips. Cover and refrigerate until ready to cook.

Remove roast and keep warm; add broth and remaining water to pan. Bring to a boil; add noodles. Cook for 8-10 minutes or until tender. Drain; season with pepper. Serve with the roast. **Yield:** 8 servings.

Editor's Note: Uncooked noodles may be stored in the refrigerator for 2-3 days or frozen for up to 1 month.

Classic Beef and Veggies

Jan Roat, Grass Range, Montana

After our children grew up and left home, I still enjoyed making this dinner.

- 1 boneless beef sirloin tip *or* 1 beef bottom round roast (about 2 pounds)
- 2 medium potatoes, cut into chunks
- 2 medium carrots, cut into 2-inch chunks
- 1 medium onion, cut into wedges
- 1/4 teaspoon pepper
- 1 can (14-1/2 ounces) Italian stewed tomatoes, undrained
- 1 can (10-3/4 ounces) condensed cream of mushroom soup, undiluted
- 1/2 cup water

Place meat in an ovenproof skillet or Dutch oven. Add the potatoes, carrots and onion. Sprinkle with pepper. Top with tomatoes. Spread soup over meat. Pour water around vegetables. Cover and bake at 325° for 1-1/2 hours or until meat and vegetables are tender. Thicken cooking liquid if desired. **Yield:** 6-8 servings.

Flavorful Pot Roast

Arlene Kay Butler, Ogden, Utah

I use my slow cooker to prepare this succulent pot roast. Convenient packages of salad dressing and gravy combine to create a tasty sauce. For a filling meal in one, I like to serve it over mashed potatoes.

- 2 boneless beef chuck roasts (2-1/2 pounds *each*)
- 1 envelope ranch salad dressing mix
- 1 envelope Italian salad dressing mix
- 1 envelope brown gravy mix
- 1/2 cup water

Place the chuck roasts in a 5-qt. slow cooker. In a small bowl, combine the salad dressing and gravy mixes; stir in water. Pour over meat. Cover and cook on low for 7-8 hours or until tender. If desired, thicken cooking juices for gravy. **Yield:** 12-15 servings.

Quick Tip

Leftover beef roast is terrific when set in the food processor and turned into barbecue sandwiches. Just add barbecue sauce and a few drops of Worcestershire sauce and serve on buns.

Flavorful Pot Roast

4 garlic cloves, minced
1 large onion, thinly sliced
1 fresh beef brisket (4 pounds)
1/2 teaspoon salt
1/4 teaspoon pepper
1/4 cup all-purpose flour
1/4 cup cold water
1/4 to 1/2 teaspoon browning sauce, optional
1 pound fresh mushrooms, sliced
1-1/2 cups dried cranberries

In a large bowl, combine the broth, cranberry juice concentrate, vinegar, rosemary and garlic; pour into a large roasting pan. Top with onion slices.

Season beef with salt and pepper; place fat side up in the pan. Cover and bake at 325° for 3 to 3-1/2 hours or until meat is tender.

Remove the meat and thinly slice across the grain. Cover slices and refrigerate overnight.

For gravy, skim fat from cooking juices; pour into a saucepan. Combine flour, water and browning sauce if desired until smooth; stir into cooking juices. Bring to a boil; cook and stir for 2 minutes or until thickened. Cover gravy and refrigerate.

Place beef slices in a shallow baking dish; top with mushrooms, cranberries and gravy. Cover and bake at 325° for 60-65 minutes or until heated through and mushrooms are tender. **Yield:** 10-12 servings.

Editor's Note: This is a fresh beef brisket, not corned beef. The meat comes from the first cut of the brisket.

Sweet-and-Sour Pot Roast

Sweet-and-Sour Pot Roast

Erica Warkentin, Dundas, Ontario

I was so pleased to receive this recipe since it gives pot roast a new mouth-watering flavor. I like to serve the sweet-and-tangy main dish with hot, fluffy rice.

12 small white potatoes, peeled
1 boneless beef chuck roast (about 3 pounds)
1 tablespoon vegetable oil
1 cup chopped onions
1 can (15 ounces) tomato sauce
1/4 cup packed brown sugar
2 to 3 tablespoons Worcestershire sauce
2 tablespoons cider vinegar
1 teaspoon salt

Place potatoes in a 5-qt. slow cooker. Trim fat from roast; brown in hot oil on all sides in a skillet. Place meat in the slow cooker. Discard all but 1 tablespoon drippings from skillet; saute onion until tender. Stir in tomato sauce, brown sugar, Worcestershire sauce, vinegar and salt. Pour over the meat and potatoes.

Cover and cook on high for 4-5 hours or until the meat is tender. Before serving, pour sauce into a skillet. Cook and stir over medium-high heat until thickened; serve with potatoes and meat. **Yield:** 6-8 servings.

Cranberry-Mushroom Beef Brisket

Margaret Welder, Madrid, Iowa

I quickly fell for this fantastic, tasty brisket when I had it at a family wedding reception. Since the meat needs to be refrigerated overnight after it bakes, it is a great make-ahead entree.

2 cups beef broth
1/2 cup cranberry juice concentrate
1/4 cup red wine vinegar
4-1/2 teaspoons chopped fresh rosemary or 1-1/2 teaspoons dried rosemary, crushed

Cranberry-Mushroom Beef Brisket

No-Fuss Beef Roast

No-Fuss Beef Roast

Lise Thomson, Magrath, Alberta

For Christmas dinner or other special occasions, this beef rib roast makes an elegant entree. I just coat the beef with a four-ingredient dry rub to spark the flavor, then stick it in the oven. If you ask me, it comes out perfect every time!

1-1/2 teaspoons seasoned salt
  1 teaspoon garlic powder
1/2 teaspoon onion powder
1/4 teaspoon cayenne pepper
  1 beef rib roast (4 to 6 pounds)
1/2 cup butter

Combine the first four ingredients; rub over roast. Place roast, fat side up, in a roasting pan. Dot with butter. Bake, uncovered, at 350° for 1-3/4 to 3 hours or until meat reaches desired doneness (for medium-rare, a meat thermometer should read 145°; medium, 160°; well-done, 170°). Let stand for 10-15 minutes before carving. Thicken pan drippings for gravy if desired. **Yield:** 6-8 servings.

   Editor's Note: One envelope of meat marinade seasoning mix may be substituted for the seasoned salt, garlic powder, onion powder and cayenne.

Old-World Sauerbraten

Phyllis Berenson, Cincinnati, Ohio

The secret to this sauerbraten is that it doesn't require marinating. It's an excellent family supper, and you can also serve it to company along with potato pancakes, red cabbage and applesauce.

  2 tablespoons vegetable oil
  1 beef rump roast (5 to 6 pounds)
  2 onions, sliced
  1 cup white vinegar
  2 cups water
1/4 cup lemon juice
  3 bay leaves
  6 whole cloves
  2 teaspoons salt
1/2 teaspoon pepper
  4 to 5 tablespoons ketchup
 12 gingersnap cookies, crumbled

In a Dutch oven, heat oil over medium-high. Brown beef on all sides. Add all remaining ingredients except gingersnaps; bring to a boil. Reduce heat; cover and simmer until beef is tender, about 3 hour.

   During the last 30 minutes, stir in gingersnaps. Remove meat; discard bay leaves and cloves. While slicing meat, bring gravy to a boil to reduce and thicken. **Yield:** 14-16 servings.

Roast Beef With Peppers

Jeanne Murray, Scottsbluff, Nebraska

This moist, flavorful entree gets a bit of Italian flair from oregano and garlic. The sauteed peppers not only are a fresh-tasting accompaniment to the meat, but they look beautiful arranged around the sliced roast on a platter.

  1 boneless rump roast (3 pounds)
  3 tablespoons vegetable oil
  3 cups hot water
  4 teaspoons beef bouillon granules
  1 tablespoon dried oregano
  1 to 2 garlic cloves, minced
1/2 teaspoon salt
1/2 teaspoon pepper
  3 medium bell peppers, julienned
  3 tablespoons butter

In a Dutch oven, brown roast on all sides in oil over medium-high heat; drain. Combine the water, bouillon, oregano, garlic, salt and pepper; pour over roast.

   Cover and bake at 350° for 3 hours or until meat is tender. Remove roast to a warm serving platter. Let stand 10 minutes before slicing.

   Meanwhile, in a large skillet, saute peppers in butter until tender. Serve peppers and pan juices with the roast. **Yield:** 8-10 servings.

Old-World Sauerbraten

Southern Pot Roast

Amber Zurbrugg, Alliance, Ohio

Cajun seasoning adds kick to this tender beef roast that's served with a corn and tomato mixture. It is a change of pace dish that's full of flavor.

    1   boneless beef chuck roast
        (2-1/2 pounds)
    1   tablespoon Cajun seasoning
    1   package (9 ounces) frozen corn,
        thawed
  1/2   cup chopped onion
  1/2   cup chopped green pepper
    1   can (14-1/2 ounces) diced
        tomatoes, undrained
  1/2   teaspoon pepper
  1/2   teaspoon hot pepper sauce

Cut roast in half; place in a 5-qt. slow cooker. Sprinkle with Cajun seasoning. Top with corn, onion and green pepper. Combine the tomatoes, pepper and hot pepper sauce; pour over vegetables.

Cover and cook on low for 5-6 hours or until meat is tender. Serve corn mixture with slotted spoon. **Yield:** 5 servings.

Country-Style Pot Roast

Country-Style Pot Roast

Joan Best, Garrison, Montana

My husband goes deer hunting, so I have quite a few recipes for venison. This is his favorite. We also like it with beef.

    2   cups water
    2   cups cider vinegar
    6   medium onions, thinly sliced
   12   whole peppercorns
    4   bay leaves
    4   whole cloves
    2   teaspoons salt
    1   teaspoon Worcestershire sauce
  1/2   teaspoon garlic powder
  1/2   teaspoon pepper
    1   boneless beef *or* venison rump
        or chuck roast (3-1/2 to 4
        pounds)
    2   tablespoons vegetable oil
   10   medium carrots, cut into 1-inch
        chunks
    5   to 7 tablespoons cornstarch
  1/3   cup cold water

In a large resealable plastic bag, combine the first 10 ingredients. Add roast. Cover and refrigerate for 24 hours.

Remove roast, reserving marinade. In a Dutch oven, brown roast in oil; drain. Add carrots and reserved marinade; bring to a rolling boil. Reduce heat; cover and simmer for 3-1/2 to 4 hours or until meat is tender.

Remove roast and keep warm. Strain cooking juices; discard vegetables and spices. Return juices to pan. Combine cornstarch and cold water until smooth; gradually add to pan juices. Bring to a boil; cook and stir for 2 minutes or until thickened. Slice roast; serve with gravy. **Yield:** 6-8 servings.

Prime Rib and Potatoes

Prime Rib And Potatoes

Richard Fairchild, Tustin, California

I've discovered a variety of small roasts that work well for two, without creating leftovers for the rest of the week. This prime rib is perfect for a nice meal when you're not expecting company. The portion for each is generous, and the aroma is unsurpassed.

    1   tablespoon olive oil
    1   small garlic clove, minced
    1   standing beef rib roast (about
        3 pounds and 2 ribs)
    2   large baking potatoes

Combine the oil and garlic; rub evenly over roast. Place roast, fat side up, in a small roasting pan. Place a potato on each side of roast. Bake, uncovered, at 325° for 2 to 2-1/2 hours until meat reaches desired doneness (for medium-rare, a meat thermometer should read 145°; medium, 160°; well done, 170°). Let stand for 10 minutes before carving. **Yield:** 2 servings.

Seasoned Rib Roast

Seasoned Rib Roast

Evelyn Gebhardt, Kasilof, Alaska

Gravy made from the drippings of this boneless beef rib roast is exceptional. You can also use a rib eye roast with excellent results.

1-1/2 teaspoons lemon-pepper seasoning

1-1/2 teaspoons paprika

3/4 teaspoon garlic salt

1/2 teaspoon dried rosemary, crushed

1/4 teaspoon cayenne pepper

1 boneless beef rib roast (3 to 4 pounds)

In a small bowl, combine the seasonings; rub over roast. Place roast fat side up on a rack in a shallow roasting pan. Bake, uncovered, at 350° for 1-3/4 to 2-1/2 hours or until meat reaches desired doneness (for medium-rare, a meat thermometer should read 145°; medium, 160°; well-done, 170°). Remove to a warm serving platter. Let stand for 10-15 minutes before carving. **Yield:** 6-8 servings.

Quick Tip

Feel free to experiment with the recipe for Seasoned Rib Roast. Replace the rosemary, for instance, with a little marjoram or thyme. Or, leave out the cayenne if you would like.

Swiss Pot Roast

Darlene Brenden, Salem, Oregon

This satisfying recipe creates such a tender roast. The potatoes and carrots make it particularly hearty and add delicious taste.

1 boneless beef chuck roast (3 pounds)

1 tablespoon vegetable oil

8 medium potatoes, peeled and quartered

8 medium carrots, cut into chunks

1 medium onion, sliced

3 tablespoons all-purpose flour

1 cup water

1 can (8 ounces) tomato sauce

1 teaspoon beef bouillon granules

1/2 teaspoon salt

1/2 teaspoon pepper

In a Dutch oven, brown roast on all sides in oil; drain. Add the potatoes, carrots and onion.

In a bowl, combine the flour, water, tomato sauce, bouillon, salt and pepper until smooth. Pour over the roast and vegetables.

Cover and bake at 325° for 2-1/2 to 3 hours or until the meat is tender. **Yield:** 8 servings.

Red-Eye Beef

Carol Stevens, Basye, Virginia

The addition of hot sauce zips up this cut of meat. It takes me back to spicy dinners I enjoyed as a child in the Southwest. I like to use the extras in different dishes—including quesadillas, burritos and even satisfying barbecued beef sandwiches.

1 boneless beef eye of round roast (about 3 pounds)

1 tablespoon vegetable oil

2-1/2 cups water, *divided*

1 envelope onion soup mix

3 tablespoons cider vinegar

2 tablespoons Louisiana hot sauce

2 tablespoons all-purpose flour

In a Dutch oven, brown roast on all sides in oil over medium-high heat; drain. Combine 3/4 cup water, soup mix, vinegar and hot sauce; pour over the roast.

Cover and bake at 325° for 2-3 hours or until tender. Transfer to a serving platter and keep warm. Let stand for 10-15 minutes before slicing.

For gravy, combine flour and remaining water until smooth; stir into meat juices. Bring to a boil; cook and stir for 2 minutes or until thickened. Serve with meat. **Yield:** 10-12 servings.

Swiss Pot Roast

Sausage Cheese Manicotti (p. 10

Chapter 6

Other Specialties

All it takes is some ground beef, steak strips or potatoes to create a variety of filling, home-cooked foods. Zesty steak fajitas, meaty lasagnas and piled-high sandwiches are just a sampling of the following stick-to-your-ribs favorites that your family will request time and again.

Steak Fajitas

Shirley Hilger, Lincoln, Nebraska

Juicy strips of sirloin pick up plenty of spicy flavor from a marinade seasoned with cayenne pepper and cumin. These colorful sandwiches are quick and satisfying.

 Uses less fat, sugar or salt. Includes Nutrition Facts.

1/4	cup orange juice
1/4	cup white vinegar
4	garlic cloves, minced
1	teaspoon seasoned salt
1	teaspoon dried oregano
1	teaspoon ground cumin
1/4	teaspoon cayenne pepper
1	pound boneless beef sirloin steak, cut into 1/4-inch strips
1	medium onion, thinly sliced
1	medium green pepper, thinly sliced
1	medium sweet red pepper, thinly sliced
2	tablespoons vegetable oil, divided
4	to 6 flour tortillas (10 inches), warmed

Shredded cheddar cheese, picante sauce and sour cream, optional

In a large resealable plastic bag, combine the orange juice, vinegar, garlic and seasonings; add the beef. Seal bag and turn to coat; set aside. In a skillet, saute onion and peppers in 1 tablespoon oil until crisp-tender; remove and set aside.

Drain and discard marinade. In the same skillet, cook beef in remaining oil for 2-4 minutes or until it reaches desired doneness. Return vegetables to pan; heat through. Spoon meat and vegetables onto tortillas. If desired, top with cheese and serve with picante sauce and sour cream. **Yield:** 4-6 servings.

Nutrition Facts: 1 fajita equals 305 calories, 11 g fat (3 g saturated fat), 42 mg cholesterol, 422 mg sodium, 27 g carbohydrate, 5 g fiber, 19 g protein.

Steak over Potatoes

Dennis Robinson, Laurel, Montana

I enjoy preparing this dish since it is one of the easiest meals I serve...so tasty, too. The chicken gumbo soup adds a unique flavor to the rest of the ingredients.

2-1/2	pounds beef round steak
1	can (10-3/4 ounces) condensed cream of onion soup, undiluted
1	can (10-1/2 ounces) condensed chicken gumbo soup, undiluted
1/4	teaspoon pepper
8	baking potatoes

Cut steak into 3-in. x 1/4-in. strips; place in a bowl. Stir in soups and pepper.

Transfer to a greased 2-1/2-qt. baking dish. Cover and bake at 350° for 30 minutes. Add potatoes to the oven. Bake for 1-1/2 hours or until meat and potatoes are tender. Serve steak over potatoes. **Yield:** 8 servings.

Steak over Potatoes

Steak 'n' Vegetable Soup

Edie DeSpain, Logan, Utah

This chunky soup calls for a lot of fresh herbs to enhance the flavor of the other ingredients. The aroma while it is cooking is absolutely wonderful. I like to serve steaming bowls of this soup alongside a green salad and baking powder biscuits.

1	pound boneless beef sirloin steak, cut into 1/2-inch cubes
1	cup chopped onion
2	teaspoons canola oil
2	cups cubed red potatoes
1	cup chopped carrots
1	cup frozen peas
1	can (14-1/2 ounces) beef broth
1	cup water
2	tablespoons balsamic vinegar
1	tablespoon minced fresh parsley
1	tablespoon minced chives
1-1/2	teaspoons minced fresh basil *or* 1/2 teaspoon dried basil
1	teaspoon minced fresh thyme *or* 1/4 teaspoon dried thyme
3/4	teaspoon salt
1/4	teaspoon pepper

In a large saucepan, cook beef and onion in oil until meat is no longer pink; drain. Stir in the potatoes, carrots and peas. Add the broth, water, vinegar, parsley, chives, basil, thyme, salt and pepper. Bring to a boil. Reduce heat; cover and simmer for 20-30 minutes or until meat and vegetables are tender. **Yield:** 6 servings.

Steak Fajitas

Meatball Pizza

Meatball Pizza

Mary Humeniuk-Smith, Perry Hall, Maryland

I always keep extra meatballs and bread shell crusts in the freezer to make this speedy pizza at the spur of the moment. Add a tossed salad and you have a delicious dinner that is ready in no time.

> 1 prebaked Italian bread shell crust (14 ounces)
> 1 can (8 ounces) pizza sauce
> 1 teaspoon garlic powder
> 1 teaspoon Italian seasoning
> 1/4 cup grated Parmesan cheese
> 1 small onion, halved and sliced
> 12 frozen fully cooked Italian meatballs, thawed and halved
> 1 cup (4 ounces) shredded part-skim mozzarella cheese
> 1 cup (4 ounces) shredded cheddar cheese

Place the crust on an ungreased 12-in. pizza pan. Spread with pizza sauce; top with garlic powder, Italian seasoning, Parmesan cheese and onion. Arrange the meatball halves over top; sprinkle with cheeses.

Bake at 350° for 12-17 minutes or until heated through and cheese is melted. **Yield:** 6-8 slices.

Sausage Potato Skillet

Eggs in the morning just aren't the same without hearty sausages and potatoes. Here, these two favorite breakfast side dishes are cooked in the same skillet, so you only dirty one pan. The recipe comes from our Test Kitchen.

> 1 package (8 ounces) brown-and-serve sausage links
> 2 tablespoons water
> 2 tablespoons vegetable oil
> 3 cups frozen shredded hash brown potatoes
> 1/2 cup chopped sweet red *or* green pepper
> 1/4 cup chopped onion
> Salt and pepper to taste

Cut sausage links into bite-size pieces. In a covered skillet, cook the sausage in water and oil over medium heat for 5 minutes. Remove sausage with a slotted spoon and keep warm.

Carefully add the potatoes, red pepper and onion to the pan. Cover and cook for 5 minutes. Uncover; cook 5-6 minutes longer or until potatoes are tender. Return sausage to pan; heat through. **Yield:** 4 servings.

Mini Chimichangas

Kathy Rogers, Hudson, Ohio

Guests will rave over this south-of-the-border specialty! Filling enough to serve as a meal, these savory wraps draw many compliments whenever I prepare them.

> 1 pound ground beef
> 1 medium onion, chopped
> 1 envelope taco seasoning
> 3/4 cup water
> 3 cups (12 ounces) shredded Monterey Jack cheese
> 1 cup (8 ounces) sour cream
> 1 can (4 ounces) chopped green chilies, drained
> 1 package (1 pound) egg roll wrappers (14 count)
> 1 egg white, lightly beaten
> Vegetable oil for frying
> Salsa and additional sour cream

In a skillet, cook beef and onion over medium heat until meat is no longer pink; drain. Stir in taco seasoning and water. Bring to a boil. Reduce heat; simmer, uncovered, for 5 minutes, stirring occasionally. Remove from the heat; cool slightly.

In a bowl, combine the cheese, sour cream and chilies. Stir in beef mixture. Place an egg roll wrapper on work surface with one point facing you. Place 1/3 cup filling in center. Fold bottom third of wrapper over filling; fold in sides. Brush top point with egg white; roll up to seal. Repeat with remaining wrappers and filling. (Keep remaining egg roll wrappers covered with waxed paper to avoid drying out.)

In a large saucepan, heat 1 in. of oil to 375°. Fry chimichangas for 1-1/2 minutes on each side or until golden brown. Drain on paper towels. Serve chimichanga warm with salsa and sour cream. **Yield:** 14 servings.

Sausage Potato Skillet

Shredded Beef Sandwiches

Nacho Meatballs

June Clark, Clarkrange, Tennessee

One day, I didn't have time to cook spaghetti sauce for my meatballs. So I used canned soup as a substitute. This dish has a great cheesy flavor and a little crunch from the french-fried onions. It can either be served as an appetizer or a main dish.

- 2 **eggs**
- 1/2 **cup ketchup**
- 1 **large onion, chopped**
- 2/3 **cup crushed saltines**
- 1/2 **cup mashed potato flakes**
- 1/2 **teaspoon garlic powder**
- 1/4 **teaspoon pepper**
- 2 **pounds lean ground beef**
- 1 **can (11 ounces) condensed nacho cheese soup, undiluted**
- 1 **can (10-3/4 ounces) condensed cream of mushroom soup, undiluted**
- 1-1/3 **cups water**
- 1 **can (2.8 ounces) french-fried onions**

In a large bowl, combine the first seven ingredients. Crumble beef over mixture; mix well. Shape into 1-1/2-in. balls.

Place meatballs on a greased rack in a shallow baking pan. Bake, uncovered, at 350° for 1 hour, turning once; drain. Combine soups and water; pour over meatballs. Sprinkle with onions. Bake 30 minutes longer or until meat is no longer pink. **Yield:** 30 meatballs.

Shredded Beef Sandwiches

Myra Innes, Auburn, Kansas

It's easy to feed a crowd with this tender and tasty beef on hamburger buns. The recipe came from my grandchildren's third grade teacher, and it remains one of our favorites.

✓ *Uses less fat, sugar or salt. Includes Nutrition Facts and Diabetic Exchanges.*

- 1 **boneless beef roast (3 pounds)**
- 1 **medium onion, chopped**
- 1/3 **cup white vinegar**
- 3 **bay leaves**
- 1/2 **teaspoon salt, optional**
- 1/4 **teaspoon ground cloves**
- 1/8 **teaspoon garlic powder**
- 12 **hamburger buns, split**

Cut roast in half; place in a 3-qt. slow cooker. Combine onion, vinegar, bay leaves, salt if desired, cloves and garlic powder; pour over roast. Cover and cook on low for 10-12 hours or until the meat is very tender. Discard bay leaves. Remove meat and shred with a fork. Serve on buns. **Yield:** 12 servings.

Nutrition Facts: 1/2 cup serving (prepared without salt and calculated without bun) equals 173 calories, 6 g fat (0 saturated fat), 78 mg cholesterol, 52 mg sodium, 2 g carbohydrate, 0 fiber, 26 g protein. **Diabetic Exchange:** 3 lean meat.

Sausage Pepper Sandwiches

Suzette Gessel, Albuquerque, New Mexico

Peppers and onions add a fresh taste to this zippy sausage filling for sandwiches. My mother gave me this recipe. It's simple to assemble, and it's gobbled up quickly.

- 5 **uncooked Italian sausage links (about 20 ounces)**
- 1 **medium green pepper, cut into 1-inch pieces**
- 1 **large onion, cut into 1-inch pieces**
- 1 **can (8 ounces) tomato sauce**
- 1/8 **teaspoon pepper**
- 6 **hoagie *or* submarine sandwich buns, split**

In a large skillet, brown sausage links over medium heat. Cut links into 1/2-in. slices; place in a 3-qt. slow cooker.

Stir in the green pepper, onion, tomato sauce and pepper. Cover and cook on low for 8 hours or until sausage is no longer pink and vegetables are tender. Use a slotted spoon to serve on buns. **Yield:** 6 servings.

Sausage Pepper Sandwiches

Asian Beef Noodles

Asian Beef Noodles

Margery Bryan, Royal City, Washington

We've raised beef the majority of our lives, so I like to try new recipes that feature it. This recipe is different and absolutely delicious.

- 1 package (3 ounces) beef-flavored ramen noodles
- 1 pound boneless beef sirloin steak (3/4 inch thick)
- 1 jalapeno pepper, seeded and finely chopped
- 1 tablespoon vegetable oil
- 2 tablespoons water
- 1 tablespoon steak sauce
- 1 medium carrot, shredded
- 2 tablespoons sliced green onion
- 1/4 cup peanut halves

Set aside the seasoning packet from the noodles. Prepare noodles according to package directions; drain and set them aside.

Cut steak into 3-in. x 1/2-in. strips. In a large skillet, stir-fry the beef and jalapeno in oil for 1-2 minutes or until meat is no longer pink. Remove and keep warm.

In the same skillet, combine the noodles, water, steak sauce, carrot, onion and contents of seasoning packet. Cook and stir until heated through. Return beef to the pan. Sprinkle with peanut halves. Serve immediately. **Yield:** 4 servings.

Editor's Note: When cutting or seeding hot peppers, use rubber or plastic gloves to protect your hands. Avoid touching your face.

Mozzarella Beef Sandwiches

Erica Svejda, Janesville, Wisconsin

This is a great supper when we're short on time. For this fantastic four-ingredient sandwich, I simply jazz up deli roast beef with cheese and jarred spaghetti sauce.

- 1 loaf (1 pound, 20 inches) unsliced French bread
- 1-1/4 pounds thinly sliced deli roast beef
- 1 cup meatless spaghetti sauce
- 1-1/4 cups (5 ounces) shredded part-skim mozzarella cheese

Cut French bread in half lengthwise; cut widthwise into five portions. On each bread bottom, layer roast beef, spaghetti sauce and cheese.

Place on an ungreased baking sheet. Broil 4 in. from the heat for 1-2 minutes or until cheese is melted; replace tops. **Yield:** 5 servings.

Quick Tip

If you make a big batch of soup, freeze the leftovers in individual servings. Line bowls with plastic wrap, pour soup and freeze. Once frozen, remove the soup from the bowls and store in large freezer bags.

Philly Cheesesteak Pizza

Anne Zirkle, South Riding, Virginia

This pizza is an ideal busy weeknight recipe. I like to add mushrooms to this tasty combination of my husband's favorite foods—pizza and Philly cheesesteaks!

- 1 prebaked Italian bread shell crust (16 ounces)
- 1 medium onion, thinly sliced and separated into rings
- 1 small sweet red pepper, cut into 1/8-inch strips
- 2 garlic cloves, minced
- 1 tablespoon olive oil
- 1/2 pound thinly sliced deli roast beef, cut into 1/4-inch strips
- 1 jar (6 ounces) sliced mushrooms, drained
- 1 teaspoon dried oregano
- 1 teaspoon dried basil
- 1/4 teaspoon salt
- 1/4 teaspoon pepper
- 1 cup (4 ounces) shredded part-skim mozzarella cheese
- 1/2 cup shredded Parmesan cheese

Place crust on a 14-in. pizza pan; set aside. In a skillet, saute the onion, red pepper and garlic in oil for 3-5 minutes or until crisp-tender. Add beef and mushrooms; cook and stir for 3-5 minutes or until heated through. Drain. Stir in the seasonings.

Spread meat mixture over crust to within 1/2 in. of edge. Combine the cheeses; sprinkle over pizza. Bake at 350° for 15 minutes or until the crust is golden and the cheese is melted. Cut into wedges. **Yield:** 4-6 servings.

Mozzarella Beef Sandwiches

Hearty Chili Mac

Fannie Wehmas, Saxon, Wisconsin

Luckily, this recipe makes a lot, since everyone always asks for a second bowl. It freezes well and makes excellent leftovers, making dinner the next day a snap.

- 2 **pounds ground beef**
- 1 **medium onion, chopped**
- 1 **can (46 ounces) tomato juice**
- 1 **can (28 ounces) diced tomatoes, undrained**
- 2 **celery ribs without leaves, chopped**
- 3 **tablespoons brown sugar**
- 2 **tablespoons chili powder**
- 1 **teaspoon salt**
- 1 **teaspoon prepared mustard**
- 1/4 **teaspoon pepper**
- 2 **cans (16 ounces *each*) kidney beans, rinsed and drained**
- 1/2 **cup uncooked elbow macaroni**

In a Dutch oven or large kettle, cook beef and onion over medium heat until meat is no longer pink; drain. Stir in the tomato juice, tomatoes, celery, brown sugar, chili powder, salt, mustard and pepper. Bring to a boil. Reduce heat; simmer, uncovered, for 1 hour, stirring occasionally.

Add the beans and macaroni; simmer 15-20 minutes longer or until macaroni is tender. **Yield:** 10-12 servings.

Hearty Chili Mac

Broiled Pizza Burgers

Broiled Pizza Burgers

Ann Bailes, Anderson, South Carolina

My mother made these open-face sandwiches when I was growing up. They're even faster to fix if you use pre-browned hamburger from the freezer. We sometimes substitute slices of cheddar for the process cheese.

- 1 **pound ground beef**
- 1 **tablespoon chopped onion**
- 2 **teaspoons cornstarch**
- 1 **can (14-1/2 ounces) diced tomatoes, undrained**
- 1 **teaspoon dried oregano**
- 1/4 **teaspoon salt**
- 1/4 **teaspoon onion salt**
- 10 **slices process cheese (Velveeta), *divided***
- 4 **hamburger buns, split**

In a large skillet, cook beef and onion over medium heat until meat is no longer pink; drain. Sprinkle with cornstarch; stir until blended. Stir in the tomatoes, oregano, salt and onion salt. Cook, uncovered, for 5 minutes or until slightly thickened. Add six cheese slices; cook and stir until cheese is melted and blended.

Place hamburger buns cut side up on an ungreased baking sheet; spoon about 1/4 cup meat mixture onto each bun half. Cut remaining cheese slices in half diagonally; place over meat mixture. Broil 6-8 in. from the heat for 4 minutes or until cheese is melted. **Yield:** 4 servings.

Steak Hash

**Barbara Nowakowski
North Tonawanda, New York**

Give leftover steak and baked potatoes a flavorful face-lift with this delicious idea. Green pepper, onion, and garlic powder lend just enough seasoning to the easy brunch dish.

- 1 **medium green pepper, chopped**
- 1 **small onion, chopped**
- 2 **tablespoons vegetable oil**
- 3 **medium potatoes (about 1 pound), peeled, cooked and diced**
- 1 **cup diced cooked steak**
- 1/4 **to 1/2 teaspoon garlic powder**

Salt and pepper to taste

- 1/4 **cup shredded Monterey Jack cheese**
- 4 **eggs**

In a skillet, saute the green pepper and onion in oil until tender. Stir in potatoes. Reduce heat; cover and cook over low heat for 10 minutes or until the potatoes are heated through, stirring occasionally.

Add steak, garlic powder, salt and pepper. Sprinkle with cheese. Cover and cook on low 5 minutes longer or until heated through and cheese is melted; keep warm.

Prepare eggs as desired. Divide hash between four plates and top with an egg. **Yield:** 4 servings.

Meatball Lasagna

Meatball Lasagna

Addella Thomas, Mt. Sterling, Illinois

I crumble extra meatballs into the homemade spaghetti sauce I use in this cheesy lasagna. My family wants me to make this dish all the time. It goes over well at family reunions, too.

    2   cans (14-1/2 ounces *each*) diced
        tomatoes, undrained
    1   can (8 ounces) tomato sauce
    1   cup water
    1   can (6 ounces) tomato paste
    1   medium onion, chopped
    1   garlic clove, minced
    1   tablespoon dried basil
    4   teaspoons dried parsley flakes
    2   teaspoons sugar
Garlic salt to taste
    8   uncooked lasagna noodles
   24   cooked meatballs
    1   egg
    1   cup ricotta cheese
    2   cups (8 ounces) shredded
        part-skim mozzarella cheese
  3/4   cup grated Parmesan cheese

In a large saucepan, combine the first 10 ingredients. Bring to a boil. Reduce heat; cover and simmer for 20 minutes. Meanwhile, cook lasagna noodles according to the package directions; drain.

Crumble meatballs into the sauce. In a small bowl, combine the egg and ricotta cheese. Spoon 1 cup of the meat sauce into a greased 13-in. x 9-in. x 2-in. baking dish. Layer with half of the noodles, ricotta mixture, meat sauce, mozzarella and Parmesan cheeses. Repeat layers.

Cover and bake at 350° for 45 minutes. Uncover; bake 5-10 minutes longer or until golden brown. Let stand for 15 minutes before cutting. **Yield:** 8-10 servings.

Sausage Potato Medley

Marie Clouse, Hope, Indiana

We raise our own meat and vegetables on our farm. I had few recipes that used sausage, so I developed this one. Wherever I serve it to friends and family, everyone asks me for the recipe.

    4   cups thinly sliced peeled
        potatoes
    1   pound bulk pork sausage
  3/4   cup chopped onion
    1   cup (4 ounces) shredded
        cheddar cheese
    3   tablespoons butter
  1/4   cup all-purpose flour
  1/2   teaspoon salt
  1/4   teaspoon pepper
    2   cups milk

Place potatoes in a saucepan and cover with water; cover and bring to a boil over medium-high heat. Cook for 5 minutes. Drain; place potatoes in a greased 2-qt. baking dish.

In a large skillet, cook sausage and onion over medium heat until meat is no longer pink; drain. Spoon over potatoes; sprinkle with cheese.

In a large saucepan, melt butter; stir in flour, salt and pepper until smooth. Gradually add milk. Bring to a boil; cook and stir for 2 minutes or until thickened and bubbly. Pour over cheese.

Cover and bake at 350° for 45-50 minutes or until potatoes are tender. **Yield:** 4-6 servings.

Italian Meatball Sandwiches

Frozen meatballs and store-bought spaghetti sauce are the time-saving tricks to these quick and filling sandwiches. Whip them up and watch them disappear!

    2   packages (12 ounces *each*)
        frozen Italian meatballs
    1   jar (28 ounces) spaghetti sauce
  3/4   cup sliced fresh mushrooms
  3/4   cup chopped green pepper
    6   hoagie *or* submarine buns, split

Place meatballs in a microwave-safe dish. Cover and microwave on high for 1-2 minutes or until slightly thawed.

Transfer meatballs to a large saucepan; add the spaghetti sauce, mushrooms and green pepper. Bring to a boil. Reduce heat; simmer, uncovered, for 3-6 minutes or until the meatballs are heated through. Serve meatballs on buns. **Yield:** 6 servings.

Editor's Note: This recipe was tested in a 1,100-watt microwave.

Quick Tip

When preparing lasagna, place the cheese mixture in a large resealable plastic bag with one corner snipped off. Then squeeze the mixture out evenly onto the noodles.

Italian Meatball Sandwiches

Potato Bread

Potato Bread

Martha Clayton, Utopia, Texas

This bread's firm crust is reminiscent of old-fashioned loaves. Using some of the cooking water provides even more delicious potato flavor.

> 1 medium potato, peeled and diced
1-1/2 cups water
> 2 packages (1/4 ounce *each*) active dry yeast
1/2 cup warm water (110° to 115°)
> 1 cup warm milk (110° to 115°)
> 2 tablespoons butter, softened
> 2 tablespoons sugar
> 2 teaspoons salt
6-1/2 to 7-1/2 cups all-purpose flour
Additional all-purpose flour

Place potato and water in a saucepan; cook until very tender. Drain, reserving 1/2 cup liquid. Mash potatoes (without added milk or butter); set aside.

In a large mixing bowl, dissolve yeast in warm water. Add the milk, butter, sugar, salt, 4 cups flour, potatoes and reserved cooking liquid; beat until smooth. Stir in enough remaining flour to form a stiff dough.

Turn onto a floured surface; knead until smooth and elastic, about 6-8 minutes. Place in a greased bowl, turning once to grease top. Cover and let rise in a warm place until doubled, about 1 hour.

Punch dough down. Turn onto a lightly floured surface; divide in half. Shape into loaves. Place in two greased 9-in. x 5-in. x 3-in. loaf pans. Cover and let rise until doubled, about 30 minutes. Sprinkle lightly with additional flour. Bake at 375° for 35-40 minutes or until golden brown. Remove from pans to wire racks to cool. **Yield:** 2 loaves.

No-Noodle Lasagna

Mary Moore, Omaha, Nebraska

This tasty recipe gives you all the comforting flavors of a favorite Italian dish without the work. I seal traditional lasagna ingredients between two layers of refrigerated crescent dough for a speedy specialty that's requested time and again.

1-1/2 pounds ground beef
> 1/2 cup chopped onion
> 1 can (6 ounces) tomato paste
> 1 tablespoon dried parsley flakes
> 1/2 teaspoon dried basil
> 1/2 teaspoon dried oregano
> 1/2 teaspoon salt
> 1/2 teaspoon pepper
Dash garlic salt
> 1 egg
1-1/2 cups (12 ounces) small-curd cottage cheese
> 1/4 cup grated Parmesan cheese
> 2 tubes (8 ounces *each*) refrigerated crescent rolls
> 1/2 pound sliced part-skim mozzarella cheese
> 1 tablespoon milk
> 1 tablespoon sesame seeds

In a large skillet, cook beef and onion over medium heat until meat is no longer pink; drain. Add tomato paste and seasonings; mix well. In a bowl, combine the egg, cottage cheese and Parmesan cheese.

Roll out each tube of crescent dough between waxed paper into a 15-in. x 10-in. rectangle. Transfer one dough rectangle to a greased 15-in. x 10-in. x 1-in. baking pan. Spread with half of the meat mixture to within 1 in. of edges; top with half of the cheese mixture. Repeat meat and cheese layers.

Top with mozzarella. Carefully place second dough rectangle on top; press edges to seal. Brush with milk; sprinkle with sesame seeds. Bake, uncovered, at 350° for 25-30 minutes or until top crust is golden brown. **Yield:** 6 servings.

Corned Beef Omelet

Kitty Jones, Chicago, Illinois

I was raised on a farm, so we ate a lot of egg dishes. We usually serve this simple omelet for breakfast with toast on the side.

> 2 green onions, sliced
> 2 tablespoons butter
> 6 eggs
> 1/4 cup milk
> 1 cup cubed cooked corned beef
> 1/2 cup shredded cheddar cheese
Dash pepper

In a large skillet, saute the onions in butter. In a bowl, lightly beat eggs and milk; pour over the onions. Cook over medium heat; as the eggs set, lift edges, letting uncooked portion flow underneath.

When the eggs are nearly set, sprinkle with the corned beef, cheese and pepper. Remove from the heat; cover and let stand for 1-2 minutes or until the cheese is melted. Cut into wedges. **Yield:** 4 servings.

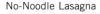
No-Noodle Lasagna

Brat 'n' Tot Bake

Stuffed Steak Rolls

These hearty beef rolls don't require a lot of fuss—they just look like they do. Use a boxed stuffing mix or leftover stuffing for the filling, then top with a tasty sauce full of onion and green pepper.

- 1 **small green pepper, cut into 1-inch pieces**
- 1 **small onion, sliced and separated into rings**
- 1 **garlic clove, minced**
- 1 **tablespoon vegetable oil**
- 3/4 **cup prepared stuffing**
- 2 **tablespoons grated Parmesan cheese**
- 2 **beef cube steaks (about 3/4 pound)**
- 1/2 **cup hot water**
- 1/2 **teaspoon beef bouillon granules**
- 1/3 **cup chili sauce**

In a skillet, saute the green pepper, onion and garlic in oil until crisp-tender; remove with a slotted spoon and set aside. Combine stuffing and cheese; spoon onto the center of the steaks. Roll up and tuck in ends; secure steak rolls with toothpicks.

In the same skillet, cook steak rolls until browned. In a bowl, combine water and bouillon; stir in chili sauce and reserved vegetable mixture. Pour over the steak rolls. Cover and simmer for 25-30 minutes or until meat is no longer pink, occasionally spooning sauce over rolls. Remove toothpicks. **Yield:** 2 servings.

Stuffed Steak Rolls

Brat 'n' Tot Bake

Jodi Gobrecht, Bucyrus, Ohio

Our town is dubbed the Bratwurst Capital of America. As a volunteer at our annual Bratwurst Festival, I could not have someone in my family who disliked bratwurst, so I developed this cheesy casserole for our son. It's the only way he will eat them.

- 1 **pound uncooked bratwurst, casings removed**
- 1 **medium onion, chopped**
- 1 **can (10-3/4 ounces) condensed cream of mushroom soup, undiluted**
- 1 **package (32 ounces) frozen Tater Tots**
- 2 **cups (16 ounces) sour cream**
- 2 **cups (8 ounces) shredded cheddar cheese**

Crumble bratwurst into a large skillet; add onion. Cook bratwurst and onion over medium heat until the meat is no longer pink; drain. Stir in the soup.

Transfer to a greased 13-in. x 9-in. x 2-in. baking dish. Top with Tater Tots and sour cream. Sprinkle with cheese. Bake, uncovered, at 350° for 35-40 minutes or until heated through and cheese is melted. Let stand for 5 minutes before serving. **Yield:** 6 servings.

Pierogi Supper

Holly Bosworth, Ocala, Florida

My husband loves pierogies, so when I needed a fast meal without a lot of cleanup, I came up with this all-in-one dinner. It's colorful, healthy and very filling.

- 1 **package (16.9 ounces) frozen pierogies**
- 2 **cups cubed fully cooked ham**
- 1 **medium yellow summer squash, cut into 1/4-inch slices**
- 1 **medium zucchini, cut into 1/4-inch slices**
- 1/2 **teaspoon garlic powder**
- 3 **tablespoons butter**

Cook pierogies according to package directions. In a large skillet, cook the ham, squash, zucchini and garlic powder in butter for 4 minutes or until squash is tender.

Drain pierogies and add to skillet; heat through. **Yield:** 4 servings.

wise, forming two triangles. Place 1 tablespoon of the beef mixture along the wide end of each triangle. Roll up; place pointed side down 2 in. apart on ungreased baking sheets. Bake at 375° for 15 minutes or until golden brown. **Yield:** 4 dozen.

Editor's Note: Mini Crescent Burgers can be assembled up to 2 hours in advance. Cover with plastic wrap and refrigerate until ready to bake.

Mountain Man Soup

Double-Crust Potato Pie

Josephine Schuemaker, York, Pennsylvania

Before my husband and I were married, my future sister-in-law made this mouth-watering Pennsylvania Dutch recipe for me. Over the years it has become one of my favorite dishes to make and enjoy.

    4   cups sliced peeled potatoes
        (1/4 inch thick)
    1   cup chicken broth
    1   medium onion, diced
    1   tablespoon butter *or* margarine
  3/4   teaspoon salt
  1/4   teaspoon pepper
Pastry for double-crust pie (9 inches)
    1   teaspoon milk

In a large saucepan, combine the potatoes, broth, onion, butter, salt and pepper. Cook, uncovered, over low heat until the potatoes are crisp-tender and the broth is absorbed, about 20 minutes; drain.

Line a 9-in. pie plate with the bottom pastry. Spoon potato mixture into the crust. Roll out remaining pastry to fit top of pie. Trim, seal and flute edges; cut vents in top. Brush with milk. Bake at 425° for 30-35 minutes or until golden brown. Serve warm. **Yield:** 6-8 servings.

Mountain Man Soup

Cordella Campbell, Rapid City, South Dakota

This chowder-like soup is sure to satisfy hearty appetites. It's chock-full of tender stew meat, fresh tomatoes, and chunks of carrot and potato, lightly seasoned with bay leaf and clove.

    1   pound stew meat
    2   tablespoons vegetable oil
    2   cups chopped celery
  2/3   cup chopped onion
  1/4   cup chopped green pepper
    2   cans (14-1/2 ounces *each*) beef
        broth
    1   can (28 ounces) diced tomatoes,
        undrained
    1   large potato, peeled and cubed
    1   large carrot, sliced
    2   teaspoons garlic salt
    1   whole clove
    1   bay leaf
  1/4   cup minced fresh parsley

In a Dutch oven, brown meat in oil; drain. Add the celery, onion and green pepper; saute for 5 minutes or until vegetables tender. Stir in the broth, tomatoes, potato, carrot, garlic salt, clove and bay leaf.

Bring to a boil. Reduce heat; simmer, uncovered, for 1 hour or until meat is tender. Discard clove and bay leaf. Stir in parsley. **Yield:** 6 servings.

Mini Crescent Burgers

Pam Buhr, Mexico, Missouri

A friend first brought these bite-size snacks to a Sunday school party. The original recipe called for pork sausage, but I substituted ground beef with taste-tempting results.

    1   pound ground beef
    1   cup (4 ounces) shredded
        cheddar cheese
    1   envelope onion soup mix
    3   tubes (8 ounces *each*)
        refrigerated crescent rolls

In a skillet, cook beef over medium heat until no longer pink; drain. Stir in the cheese and soup mix; set aside.

Separate crescent dough into triangles; cut each triangle in half length-

Mini Crescent Burgers

Bacon Potato Chowder

Bob Wedemeyer, Lynnwood, Washington

This is a true stick-to-your-ribs potato soup. In place of the bacon, you can substitute cubed cooked ham.

- 12 bacon strips, diced
- 2 medium onions, chopped
- 6 celery ribs, sliced
- 12 medium potatoes, peeled and cubed
- 1/3 cup butter
- 1 cup all-purpose flour
- 8 cups milk
- 2 medium carrots, shredded
- 1 tablespoon salt
- 1 teaspoon pepper

In a large skillet, cook bacon over medium heat until crisp. Remove bacon with a slotted spoon to paper towels. Saute onions and celery in the drippings until tender; drain.

Place potatoes in a Dutch oven and cover with water. Bring to a boil. Reduce heat; cover and cook for 20 minutes or until potatoes are tender. Drain; set potatoes aside.

In the same pan, melt butter. Stir in flour until smooth; gradually stir in milk. Bring to a boil over medium heat; cook and stir for 2 minutes or until thickened.

Reduce heat; add the onion mixture, potatoes, carrots, salt and pepper. Cook for 10 minutes or until chowder is heated through. Sprinkle chowder with bacon. **Yield:** 12-14 servings.

Warm Layered Sandwich

Warm Layered Sandwich

Warmed to perfection in the oven, this well-stacked loaf offers eight layers of classic sandwich staples, including deli turkey and ham, sliced salami and two types of cheese. If you have some extra time, our home economists suggest keeping the loaf in the oven a minute or two longer to melt the cheese to your liking.

- 1 unsliced round loaf (1 pound) Italian bread
- 2 tablespoons honey mustard
- 1/4 pound thinly sliced deli turkey
- 1/4 pound thinly sliced hard salami
- 1/4 pound sliced part-skim mozzarella cheese
- 2 thin slices red onion, separated into rings
- 1/4 pound thinly sliced deli ham
- 1/4 pound sliced Monterey Jack cheese
- 1 medium plum tomato, sliced
- 3 romaine leaves, torn

Cut bread in half. Carefully hollow out bottom and top of loaf, leaving a 3/4-in. shell (discard removed bread or save for another use). Spread mustard on cut sides of bread.

On the bread bottom, layer the turkey, salami, mozzarella cheese, onion, ham, Monterey Jack cheese and tomato. Replace top. Wrap in heavy-duty foil; place on a baking sheet. Bake at 450° for 12-15 minutes or until heated through. Place romaine over tomato. Cut into wedges. **Yield:** 6 servings.

Slow-Cooked Smokies

Sundra Hauck, Bogalusa, Louisiana

I like to include these little smokies smothered in tangy barbecue sauce on all my appetizer buffets. They are popular with both children and adults.

- 1 package (1 pound) miniature smoked sausages
- 1 bottle (28 ounces) barbecue sauce
- 1-1/4 cups water
- 3 tablespoons Worcestershire sauce
- 3 tablespoons steak sauce
- 1/2 teaspoon pepper

In a 3-qt. slow cooker, combine all ingredients; mix well. Cover and cook on low for 6-7 hours. Serve with a slotted spoon. **Yield:** 8 servings.

Slow-Cooked Smokies

Sausage Cheese Manicotti

Potato Spinach Pie

Lola Kauffmann, Goshen, Indiana

I combined two recipes to come up with this dish that's terrific for either brunch or dinner. Reduced-fat cheese, egg whites and a golden shredded-potato crust help lighten it up.

- **3** cups coarsely shredded peeled potatoes
- **2** tablespoons olive oil, *divided*
- **1** teaspoon salt, *divided*
- **1/3** cup chopped onion
- **1** package (10 ounces) frozen chopped spinach, thawed and squeezed dry
- **1** cup (4 ounces) shredded reduced-fat Swiss cheese
- **1/2** cup fat-free evaporated milk
- **2** eggs, lightly beaten
- **2** egg whites, lightly beaten
- **1/2** to 1 teaspoon dried oregano
- **1/4** teaspoon ground nutmeg

In a bowl, combine the potatoes, 4 teaspoons oil and 1/2 teaspoon salt. Press onto the bottom and up the sides of a 9-in. pie plate coated with nonstick cooking spray. Bake at 425° for 20-25 minutes or until crust is lightly browned. Cool on a wire rack. Reduce temperature to 350°.

In a nonstick skillet, saute onion in remaining oil until tender. In a bowl, combine the spinach, Swiss cheese, milk, eggs, egg whites, oregano, nutmeg, onion and remaining salt. Pour into crust.

Bake for 25-30 minutes or until top begins to brown and a knife inserted near the center comes out clean. Let stand for 10 minutes before cutting. **Yield:** 6 servings.

Potato Spinach Pie

Sausage Cheese Manicotti

This marvelous manicotti, created by our Test Kitchen staff, is cheesy, saucy and savory. Pair it with a garden-fresh tossed salad and soft, cheesy breadsticks for a delicious Italian feast.

✓ *Uses less fat, sugar or salt. Includes Nutrition Facts and Diabetic Exchanges.*

- **10** uncooked manicotti shells
- **8** ounces turkey Italian sausage links, casings removed
- **1** cup finely chopped sweet red pepper
- **1/4** cup chopped onion
- **2** egg whites
- **3** cups fat-free cottage cheese
- **1** cup (4 ounces) shredded part-skim mozzarella cheese
- **1/2** cup shredded Parmesan cheese, *divided*
- **3** tablespoons minced fresh parsley
- **1/2** teaspoon dried basil
- **1/2** teaspoon fennel seed
- **1/4** teaspoon white pepper
- **2** cups meatless spaghetti sauce
- **1/2** cup water

Cook manicotti according to package directions. Meanwhile, crumble sausage into a nonstick skillet; add the red pepper and onion. Cook over medium heat until meat is no longer pink and vegetables are tender; drain. Drain manicotti; set aside.

In a bowl, combine the sausage mixture, egg whites, cottage cheese, mozzarella cheese, 1/4 cup Parmesan cheese, parsley, basil, fennel and pepper. Stuff into manicotti shells. Combine spaghetti sauce and water; spread 1/2 cup in an ungreased 13-in. x 9-in. x 2-in. baking dish. Arrange shells over sauce; top with remaining sauce.

Cover and bake at 350° for 35-40 minutes. Uncover; sprinkle too with the remaining Parmesan cheese. Bake for 10-15 minutes longer or until cheese is melted. Let stand for 10 minutes before serving. **Yield:** 5 servings.

Nutrition Facts: 1 serving (2 stuffed shells) equals 462 calories, 13 g fat (5 g saturated fat), 51 mg cholesterol, 1,418 mg sodium, 48 g carbohydrate, 4 g fiber, 39 g protein. **Diabetic Exchanges:** 4 lean meat, 2 starch, 2 vegetable, 1/2 fat-free milk.

Sour Cream Potato Rolls

Super Sandwich

Patrice Barker, Tampa, Florida

This big meaty sandwich is one I've made many times when I knew I'd be feeding a hungry bunch. Everyone remarks on the tasty olive salad tucked between slices of meat and cheese. Since it can be made ahead, you're free to visit with family and friends.

- 1 medium cucumber, peeled, seeded and chopped
- 1 medium tomato, seeded and chopped
- 1 small onion, chopped
- 1/2 cup pitted ripe olives, chopped
- 1/2 cup pimiento-stuffed olives, chopped
- 1/4 cup prepared Italian salad dressing
- 1 round loaf (1-1/2 pounds) unsliced sourdough, white *or* whole wheat bread
- 1/2 pound sliced fully cooked ham
- 1/4 pound sliced salami
- 1/4 pound sliced cooked pork
- 1/2 pound sliced Swiss cheese
- 1/2 pound sliced Muenster cheese

In a large bowl, combine cucumber, tomato, onion, olives and salad dressing; set aside.

Cut 1 in. off the top of the bread; set aside. Carefully hollow out top and bottom of loaf, leaving a 1/2-in. shell. (Discard removed bread or save bread for another use.)

Layer a fourth of the ham, salami, pork and cheeses inside the shell. Top with third of the vegetable mixture. Repeat layers, ending with the meat and cheeses, gently pressing down to flatten as needed.

Replace bread top; wrap tightly in plastic. Refrigerate sandwich until serving. **Yield:** 8 servings.

Sour Cream Potato Rolls

Carol Giesbrecht, Kitchener, Ontario

Made with leftover mashed potatoes, these tender rolls have been a favorite in my family for years. They are delicious fresh from the oven with butter and peach jam.

- 1/2 cup sour cream
- 1/2 cup water (70° to 80°)
- 1/2 cup mashed potatoes (with added butter and milk)
- 1/4 cup butter, softened
- 2 tablespoons sugar
- 1 teaspoon salt
- 1/2 teaspoon baking soda
- 1/8 teaspoon ground mace
- 3 cups bread flour
- 3 teaspoons active dry yeast

In bread machine pan, place all ingredients in order suggested by manufacturer. Select dough setting (check the dough after 5 minutes of mixing; add 1 to 2 tablespoons of water or flour if needed).

When cycle is completed, turn dough onto a lightly floured surface. Punch dough down. Divide dough into 18 portions; roll each into a ball. Place on greased baking sheets. Cover and let rise in a warm place until doubled, about 30 minutes.

Bake at 375° for 10-15 minutes or until rolls are golden brown. Serve rolls warm. Remove to wire racks to cool. **Yield:** 1-1/2 dozen.

Teriyaki Steak Subs

Sandra Burgess, Birch Tree, Missouri

This simple crowd-pleaser layers submarine sandwich rolls with a seasoned mixture of sirloin strips, sliced peppers and sweet pineapple rings. The interesting flavors blend quite nicely.

- 1/4 cup steak sauce
- 1 tablespoon brown sugar
- 1 tablespoon soy sauce
- 1/2 teaspoon ground ginger
- 1 pound boneless beef sirloin steak, cut into 1/2-inch strips
- 1 medium sweet red pepper, thinly sliced
- 1 medium green pepper, thinly sliced
- 1 medium onion, thinly sliced
- 2 garlic cloves, minced
- 1 tablespoon vegetable oil
- 4 hoagie buns, split and toasted
- 8 pineapple slices

In a bowl, combine steak sauce, brown sugar, soy sauce and ginger; set aside. In a skillet or wok, stir-fry steak, peppers, onion and garlic in oil for 5 minutes. Stir in reserved sauce; top with pineapple. Cover and simmer for 5 minutes or until heated through. Spoon meat mixture onto rolls; top each with two pineapple slices. **Yield:** 4 servings.

Teriyaki Steak Subs

General Recipe Index

✓ *Uses less fat, sugar or salt. Includes Nutrition Facts.*

✓ *Uses less fat, sugar or salt. Includes Nutrition Facts.*

✓ *Uses less fat, sugar or salt. Includes Nutrition Facts.*

Alphabetical Index

✓ *Uses less fat, sugar or salt. Includes Nutrition Facts.*

✓ *Uses less fat, sugar or salt. Includes Nutrition Facts.*